BALANCING THE SCALE

Richard J. Jackson

authorHOUSE®

AuthorHouse™
1663 Liberty Drive
Bloomington, IN 47403
www.authorhouse.com
Phone: 1-800-839-8640

First published by AuthorHouse 9/29/2010

ISBN: 978-1-4520-6509-0 (sc)
ISBN: 978-1-4520-6510-6 (e)

Library of Congress Control Number: 2010912435

Printed in the United States of America
This book is printed on acid-free paper.

To My Wife, Linda,
For Her Patience and Kindness

CHAPTER I
BAD NEWS

"How long?" asked Evan Brinkley.

"Six months, a year at the outside," replied Dr. Grimes, the renowned cancer specialist.

"Any restrictions?"

"Let your body guide you. You'll become weaker and require increasingly long periods of rest; otherwise, you can do what you want, where and when you want."

Grimes' diagnosis came as no surprise, matching the first that he had received from another doctor six weeks ago. Evan rose slowly and shook hands respectfully with the doctor before leaving the office.

After things didn't go his way, he retreated without complaint. This encounter was no exception. Evan had always avoided confrontations and unpleasantness; consequently, he was usually engaged in inner turmoil.

In college, his teacher education major in English at the University of Idaho's main campus in Moscow was ill-considered. He received a passing grade in student teaching at the town's only high school, only after promising his supervising teacher that he would never accept a teaching position. Worse than being treated with disrespect, Evan was ignored by students and school staff. He dreaded every day of the practice teaching experience. Upon its completion, he found a technical writing job at Medfast, a growing medical supply firm in Spokane, through the University Placement Office. It was steady work and perfect cover for an introvert.

Evan met his wife at church, and surprisingly, she initiated the relationship. An MBA, June relished the control she had over Evan. He accepted the structure which she provided to his life and was pleased with her scrubbed good looks. Evan never actually proposed; June simply sent him to a mall for a ring she had already selected. He bought the ring a few weeks later and gave it to her on her next birthday. Of course, she planned the wedding. Since his parents were deceased, his only sibling, a sister living in Connecticut, attended. She did not bring her pre-school son or her husband, citing distance and cost as the prime reasons. June's family used the reception as a family reunion, ignoring both Evan and his sister. He continued to be an afterthought as his daughters were born and June built her career.

He was glad that his wife wasn't around for his final months. He could never bear disappointing her and had spent most of his spare time in their thirty years of marriage in a futile attempt to stay out of her way.

June's sudden death in an auto accident late last year had forced him to deal with demons within himself that he had previously been able to suppress. Evan had been taught to be fair to others, even if they were unfair to him. His three daughters, each in their own way, had refused to accept this approach. When seeing him get the short end, June just shrugged and went about her business.

Throughout his life, Evan had managed to deflect some of life's injustices and to accept others without fighting back. As he looked at his reflection in the glass of the Spokane hardware store window, he resolved to balance the scale. His one-hundred sixty pounds, distributed evenly over his slight five-foot ten inch frame, were unremarkable. His curly brown hair flopped lazily over his narrow forehead. Surprisingly, he noted a rare glint in his eye as he stared at his image. He felt his blood pressure rise and his senses sharpen. At once, Evan realized how he was going to spend his last months; those who had mistreated him were going to pay.

CHAPTER II
HIS REACTION

Evan drove the forty-five minutes to Lake Coeur d'Alene as he had led his life, slowly and deliberately. His body fit comfortably into the late model Accord sedan. He often listened to talk radio as he drove, but there was not much point in doing that any longer. After all, he was not even going to be around for the next election. Instead, Evan spent the drive time marveling at the beauty of the trees and the mountains. In part, he had rationalized his failure to counter life's cruelty by thinking how fortunate he was to live in this wonderful setting.

All his life, Evan had concluded that it was unreasonable to expect people's behavior to match the high caliber of these surroundings. He had now changed his mind; his new opinion was that those in his life who had made it more difficult deserved to pay for their brutality. Just thinking these thoughts caused him to set his jaw and straighten his shoulders.

Pulling onto the edge of the road which encircled the Lake, he parked and locked the car on a remote stretch of asphalt. Evan zipped his jacket against the chilly April breeze and began to walk clockwise on the trail that flanked the road. Since childhood, Evan had sought out safe places to reflect upon the world around him. He was happiest here where he could enjoy the peace and solitude.

There were important decisions to make: How far back in his life would he go to get even? What forms would his revenge take? Was he willing to break the law? How far over the line would his actions go? How many distinct acts of revenge could he fit in during the months he had remaining? What factors, if any, would cause him to be charitable and give a pass to some of his previous tormentors? What measures would he take to avoid getting caught? Did he care if he was caught?

Evan realized that he would not be able to settle each grievance; some of those responsible had passed on, others were too sick to trifle with, and still others had moved far away. He shrank the size and scope of his problems by initially choosing to settle one old score. Who better to start his crusade against than Coach Middleton?

Evan winced as painfully fresh images of the Coach's insensitive, often brutal, actions flooded his mind. Even if Middleton did not understand how he had hurt people, Evan vowed to inflict some pain upon him. This was the justice of which the Bible spoke, an eye for an eye, etc.

In crossing the road upon returning to his car, two teen-agers veered their car towards him and swore loudly before laughing and driving off quickly. Before they could get far, Evan grabbed a stone and bounced it off their back car window, something he never would have done before today. This aggressive act empowered him; Evan saw it as a good sign of things to come. He felt confident because the stone-throwing validated his new approach to life. The new Evan had taken his first step towards getting even.

Looking back, the husky youngsters slowed their car and considered turning around and engaging him, but there was something about his posture and facial expression that discouraged them. They looked at each other and drove away without speaking a word. Evan stood defiantly in the middle of the road as he watched them disappear.

CHAPTER III
COACH MIDDLETON

Evan had attended Spokane's finest college preparatory high school. With its well behaved, intelligent students, this college prep school was a favorite choice of teachers because the students were generally respectful and motivated. Teacher turnover was rare.

Coach Middleton had signed on after a mediocre football career at the University of Oregon and had been the defensive line coach of the school's run-of-the-mill high school football team for fifteen years by the time Evan was a freshman. Still wearing a crew-cut from his playing days, Middleton had become increasingly frustrated as it became clear that he would never accomplish much as a coach.

He was shown disrespect by fellow teachers and all students, players and non-players alike; he responded in kind with a glum stare and occasional acts of cruelty.

As a late-maturing freshman, Evan was unlucky enough to be in the wrong place at the wrong time. Detained by a history teacher, he had dressed hurriedly in the locker room and was running full-tilt in the hallway leading to the gym to avoid being late for Coach Middleton's class. As he entered the gym, he collided with the Coach and caught him squarely with his knee below Middleton's belt. Incensed, the Coach grabbed Evan by the neck, zipped him in a large plastic bag designed to carry footballs, and hung the bag on the hook of a storage closet door. After making sure Evan could breathe, Coach made sure he wasn't going anywhere by securing the bag with a Yale lock before going to his gym class.

Decidedly claustrophobic, Evan soiled himself. After the class ended, Coach had two of his players open the lock and let Evan out of the bag. His classmates hooted and hollered and never let him forget it. Now it was Coach Middleton's turn to be embarrassed!

Evan drove slowly around the lake, plotting his revenge. He knew that, after the coach's divorce, Middleton had moved into a fishing cabin on the road which encircled Lake Coeur D'Alene. He stopped at a cluster of mail boxes near a dumpster and found a dirty "Middleton" box with a number on it. Evan drove a short distance down the road and matched the box number with numerals on a run-down cabin under a big oak tree. Evan speculated that Middleton had chosen the cabin because of its proximity to the sleazy bar on the Lake's edge. Since it was track season, the Coach would probably not return until after dark. Evan had learned enough for now. He drove home, took a brief nap, ate lightly, and then began planning.

Evan didn't want to kill the nasty old coach, but he didn't care if he hurt him and made him very uncomfortable. Evan blamed the coach in part for his inability to connect with people.

The next day during his second ride past Middleton's rented cottage, Evan noticed a small storage building nearby. The steep spires of the building's roof presented Evan the opportunity he wanted. He gathered a 2X4, hammer and nails, a cheap flashlight, some rope and a large sea bag which had all been stored in his garage, before filling an empty quart bourbon bottle with cheap tea.

On Wednesday afternoon, he pulled past the cottage, turned, and parked down a deserted road. Carrying the sea bag over his shoulder, he doubled back to the cottage and went behind the storage building.

Satisfied that he was unobserved, Evan climbed to the roof with the aid of two old trash cans and began working. He secured the 2X4 by hammering two nails on its edges, making sure to face the bottle on the board towards Middleton's front door. Evan then looped the rope around the nails, packed the sea bag underneath the board, and placed the bottle on the board. He ran a few tests to ensure that the bag would unfurl when the bottle was lifted from the board. Evan then positioned the flashlight towards the bottle and turned the switch on. Satisfied with his work, he climbed down from the roof. The trap was set.

He drove his car one mile north to a secluded grove and hid his car carefully. Evan walked back in the lingering twilight, positioning himself behind trees as cars came down the road. Unseen, he came to a tall tree near the coach's cabin and climbed steadily to a comfortable perch near its top. Evan settled in and dozed off quickly, waking as two cars came by before the coach came home.

Clutching a carry-out bag in one hand and a gym bag in another, Middleton placed both on his front porch and fished his house key from his pocket. While glancing over his shoulder, the coach noticed the flashlight beam highlighting what looked like a bottle filled with bourbon. Never one to pass up an opportunity, he put the two bags inside the cabin and removed his ladder from the garage.

Evan watched carefully as the coach, more agile than he appeared, scaled the deeply pitched roof and yanked the bottle of tea, thereby opening the sea bag and entangling himself. The more he squirmed, the tighter the bag wrapped him. To make matters worse, the coach had turned himself upside down in his struggles and blood rushed to his head, making him light-headed. He passed out for several minutes and did not regain consciousness until it was pitch dark. The coach yelled but was unable to muster the full force of his coaching command voice because of his predicament. No one came to his aid, and he began whimpering.

Evan had seen and heard enough. Using a disguised voice, he called the coach's worst enemy, Mr. Lane, at his home and told him that there was trouble at the coach's house. Evan waited to see Mr. Lane drive up, then descended from his perch and walked back to his car. As he drove past the coach's cabin, Evan honked his horn several times, causing a neighbor to appear and look around. The neighbor apparently could now hear the coach's weak cries and see Mr. Lane prowling around the cabin. Co-workers and neighbors would soon hear all about this little episode.

Evan drove home and after taking a long shower and drinking a bottle of beer, slept his best eight hours in years. He called the school at 9 AM and asked for Coach Middleton. The coach had called in sick. Revenge was sweet!

CHAPTER IV
DAUGHTERS

At 8:30 AM, Evan woke and ate cereal, fruit, and a muffin. He looked around the house, which had been made so lively by his daughters and marked so indelibly by his wife. June ruled and he did not recall making a single decision regarding purchases or renovations for the house's interior. His four-bedroom, three-bathroom ranch sat comfortably in a cul-de-sac. There was no mortgage, and the home was in good repair. Evan quickly decided that he would not spend any of his precious time left in selling the home. When he passed, his oldest daughter could dispose of the home at her convenience.

Evan called his workplace and left a message for his boss, indicating that the original diagnosis had been confirmed and that he no longer cared to work. On a return call, Mr. Abrams suggested that he come to the office the next day for a brief acknowledgement of his years of service. Evan's initial reaction was to avoid his co-workers, but then he realized that he must start facing things if he was to exact revenge successfully. He agreed to be in Abrams' office at 11 AM.

While in telephone mode, he decided to invite his daughters and his three grandchildren to the house on Sunday afternoon and explain his situation. He called Sharon, his oldest daughter, first.

"Sharon, how are you?"

"Hi dad," she answered, sounding preoccupied. Sharon was a tall, dark, serious thirty-five year old with hall-of-fame multitasking credentials. She had recently completed an MBA in her spare time, without any apparent changes in her life. Sharon looked and acted like her mother. She had excelled in school and on the athletic field and could manage anything or anybody.

"Can you, Bill, and the girls come over on Sunday afternoon? I'm asking your sisters, too."

"We could be there by three. Rachel has a soccer game. Is there anything wrong?"

"I would like to speak with all of you at the same time," he answered, disclosing nothing.

She hesitated briefly, but then replied, "OK, see you at three."

Before signing off, he startled her by saying, "I love you," loudly and convincingly. Invariably, when he told his girls that he loved them, he sounded as though the words were painful for him.

Sharon was puzzled by his manner and considered how to handle this matter. Her husband, Bill, would not mind the visit; Bill and her dad were more alike than she cared to admit. Sarah, age 14, and Rachel, age 11, would grumble because they interpreted their grandfather's lack of emotion as a lack of love for them. Sharon would give them a pep talk and bribe the girls, if necessary; Sharon Brinkley Samuels would prevail, as usual.

Evan decided to call his middle daughter next. Mary, a pretty, athletic blonde and a decidedly free spirit, was an excellent fifth grade teacher. Sprinkled among the many unselfish things she has done for family, friends, and strangers alike, Mary had made some spectacularly bad decisions. For example, her first husband was like her first car, good-looking but not able to run well for long before breaking down. She relied more upon instinct than logic and more upon intuition than common sense.

Mary was determined to leave the world better than she found it and so far was way ahead. Since her high school prom days when she took a boy who had attempted suicide, to her current role of Big Sister in a local social program, she was rarely without a human project. Her second husband, Jack Hunter, is like her in many respects. They are fascinated by their three-year old son, Ned, who always has his questions answered and his needs met. Evan did not begin to understand any of these three but reasoned that it was unnecessary for him to do so. Unfortunately, his confusion in their presence was usually interpreted as disapproval.

When Jack answered his call, he carried on a brief conversation before asking, "Is Mary home?"

"No. Ned and I are holding the fort."

"Are the three of you busy on Sunday afternoon?"

"No," answered Jack, somewhat taken back by the question.

"I would like all of you to come over. Is that all right?"

"Sure, we'll be there."

"Please have Mary call Sharon to work out the arrangements."

"Will do. Thanks for calling."

Evan left a voicemail for Cary, his youngest, when he missed her with his call. She called back after he had sorted mail and put away dishes. Cary has been working on a nursing degree part-time and serving as a receptionist part-time in a doctor's office. She recently married Monte Woodridge, a local DJ. Evan did not find Monte's one-liners amusing or his loud clothes appropriate, but they endured each other.

"Are you and Monte available for dinner at the house on Sunday?"

"Sure. What can I bring?"

"Talk with Sharon."

"Mind if I bring my anatomy textbook? I've fallen behind."

"Of course not. See you then."

With phone in hand, Cary was transfixed for a moment because of her dad's uncharacteristically assertive manner. She shook her head in wonder before tackling her homework.

CHAPTER V
RETIREMENT PARTY

Jenny, **Mr. Abrams'** aide, greeted Evan when he got off the elevator and ushered him into Abrams' office. All three spent a full hour reviewing loose ends and establishing his final pay arrangements. Jenny wrote furiously, occasionally asking for clarifications. She was surprised by the respect her boss accorded to Evan and by the sophistication of the answers which Evan provided to complex Medfast issues. In her four years with the company, she had scarcely been aware of Evan but realized now that the company was losing a valuable employee.

After receiving Evan's assurances that he would accept phone calls and come into the office, if necessary, to resolve any problems, Mr. Abrams led Jenny and Evan into the tastefully appointed lunch room. Employees were given thirty minutes to eat in this room during one of two shifts. Years ago, Evan had switched his lunch to the quieter second shift. He preferred to eat alone, while skimming a newspaper. Evan had become almost invisible at lunch, and some of the employees needed to be reminded of his name on this, his last day of work.

There was a modest, catered buffet lunch, and employees were divided into Group A (12:15 PM) and Group B (12:45 PM), sixty to a group. In a choral seating arrangement, the employees sat at tables of five. With Mr. Abrams, Evan sat at the focus point in the room and looked around in a measured fashion, surprising himself by how confident and relaxed he felt. Before each group, Mr. Abrams introduced Evan and thanked him for his years of service.

Evan responded by saying, "I enjoyed working here. Unfortunately, a health problem prevents me from continuing." He then surprised everyone by stating that "in the future, he hoped all employees would be kind to his replacement and to each other. Our company can only be as welcoming or as productive as its most poorly treated employee."

To those who made eye contact with him after his brief statement, he stared them down defiantly. Evan surprised the handful of well wishers at the door after each session by shaking their hands firmly and thanking them by name in a clear voice. For a few brief minutes after years of anonymity, Evan was leaving a modest Medfast legacy and he enjoyed it.

There was a minor buzz as each of the two sets of employees returned to their work stations; many spoke while others just looked at each other. During this day's short lunch periods, Evan had prompted many employees to be more aware of all of their co-workers and not to underestimate anyone.

As the caterers cleared the luncheon remains, Mr. Abrams shook Evan's hand and watched in amazement as Evan left, striding purposefully with his head held high. Abrams was left wondering where this employee had been all these years. Evan never looked back.

CHAPTER VI
SUNDAY DINNER

Evan spent Saturday cleaning and shopping for the family dinner. He skipped church on Sunday and organized his thoughts on a yellow pad. Evan wanted them all to hear the same message and was particularly concerned that his grandchildren understand his situation. While Evan planned to answer all follow-up questions, he felt that if his remarks were clear, few questions would be necessary. He worked upon striking a balance between communicating fully but briefly.

Satisfied with his preparation, Evan carried an apple into his backyard and inspected the home's exterior. He felt some ownership of the home's outside because he had painted, pressure-washed and otherwise cared for its outer surface, in addition to doing the landscaping. Munching distractedly, Evan thought of how content he had been to do chores outside the home, thereby avoiding the family's complexity and intramural skirmishes. At first, he told himself that his reticence was due to gender differences but soon had to concede that it was his own problems with life's give-and-take that prompted his retreat.

Explaining that Bill and the girls would be along shortly, Sharon took over the kitchen immediately upon her arrival. She had worked out meal details with her sisters. Evan told his daughter firmly that he would wait for the rest of the family outside. As they exited their cars, he hugged or shook hands with each of them, uncharacteristically making solid eye contact in doing so.

After confirming with Sharon that dinner could wait five minutes, he slammed his hand on the kitchen counter to get everyone's attention. The children ignored their grandfather as usual, but the adults did not. The parents quieted their children while staring at Evan, who was standing ramrod straight with his hand on the kitchen counter. From his vantage point, everyone was able to see and hear him clearly.

He had purchased several clothing items to reinforce his presence. He chose a new red shirt for this occasion, and he looked at each person before speaking. No one had ever seen Evan so much in control.

"I want each of you to pay careful attention. I am going away soon and may not again have the chance to speak with all of you at the same time. Two smart doctors say that I will die before Christmas, and I have some things to do."

Mary sputtered in protest, but he held up his hand and gave her a challenging look. She dropped her eyes and settled down.

"Know that I love and respect all of you. Because I am shy, I have not been good at showing my love. Understand clearly that I am not afraid of dying."

Evan shed a few tears and looked away for a moment, and his children and grandchildren looked at each other. They had never seen him cry. He gathered himself and walked into the middle of the gathering.

"Because you are the oldest, Sharon, I ask that you be the executor of the will. I will meet with you within the next week."

"Molly, please arrange a fair distribution of the household goods and clothing."

"Cary, make my funeral arrangements."

"Please talk with me later this afternoon with any questions you may have. Right now, let's eat!"

His three children did not have questions, but his grandchildren did. They directed their concerns to their parents, while Evan spoke with his sons-in-law. Evan then caught Sharon's eye and nodded towards the kitchen. She was momentarily flustered by her father's take-charge attitude, but she and her sisters moved into the kitchen and began dinner preparations.

CHAPTER VII
MENSA MEETING

As Evan entered a meeting room in Spokane's main library, he smiled inwardly. How like him to be a member of a group of outsiders with high IQs such as those who attended the local MENSA meetings! As a group, he found them to be self-conscious and increasingly paranoid. Known as smart but weird, they were 180 degrees opposed to the expression, "comfortable in their own skin." He fit all too well.

Not even this night's forbidding topic, "Synchronizing Dissonant Elements through Triangulation," could scare away this crew; strangely, it might have been part of the attraction. As if the title wasn't daunting enough, a sign placed on an easel explained that the title's task would be accomplished through an analysis of converging elements from a Bach symphony, a random table of logarithms, and Einstein's DNA analysis.

It had taken Evan several months to realize that the presenters often were simply out to impress, rather than to inform. They usually resented questions and frequently took great pains to avoid being understood. For these presenters, widespread puzzled expressions and stunned silence were hallmarks of success.

Evan nodded to a few people he knew, while desperately hoping he would not take a seat next to someone particularly obnoxious. The six rows of eight chairs each were almost full, though it was still ten minutes before the presentation was scheduled to begin. Social situations like choosing a seat in a crowded room were often difficult for Evan. He slipped past a woman who was looking downward and sat next to her. As he settled in, she turned to him and smiled, then turned quickly away.

Her smile warmed him in a curious way and prompted him to introduce himself.

"I'm Evan Brinkley."

"I know. I'm Lindy James and I'm sorry about your wife."

"Thank you. How did you know her?"

"She hired me, but I didn't work with her directly."

"Are you still working the same job?"

"Sort of, but I'm doing contract work now."

Evan surprised himself by saying, "I would like to hear more about that," just as the moderator began to introduce the goateed speaker, Dr. Rinehart.

The professor made a convincing case for the selection of interdisciplinary majors for college students, undergraduates and graduates alike. She postulated that anything could be explained if the proper variables were selected. At that point things got murky as she analyzed the pre-selected music, mathematics, and biology variables. Dr. Rinehart fielded questions with rapid fire questions of her own. For the few in the group who learned in that modality, the presentation was a huge success. The rest, including Evan and Lindy, were left overwhelmed.

As Lindy turned to leave, Evan asked her, "Would you care to have a cup of coffee?"

"It's too late for coffee for me, but I could use a walk to clear my head. Interested?"

"Sure. Want to walk these streets? They're plenty safe."

She smiled and said that was fine with her.

The street lights cast an irregular glow over Lindy, creating shadows that were both flattering and intriguing. Evan noticed how animated she became when answering his questions.

When Evan spoke of his daughters, Lindy displayed a genuine interest. "Cary schedules my doctor's visits. She is very helpful and the patients like her."

"You must be proud of her."

"I am," he replied, somewhat hesitantly. "She is working on her nursing degree."

After learning that Cary was a year away from her degree and inquiring about her husband, she concluded, "I'm sure she will be a wonderful nurse."

After walking more than a mile, they circled back towards her car. When the conversation stopped, neither felt uncomfortable nor obliged to fill the void. This was not the dead air so frightening to radio announcers, but rather a gentle, natural ending to a nice visit. When they reached her car, she turned and thanked him for a pleasant walk.

"I would like to call you."

She gave him a business card and a warm smile. He returned her smile with a small salute with the card and walked to his car. He drove back to her parking space to make sure that she had departed safely. Lindy was gone but not forgotten.

CHAPTER VIII
CELEBRATION

Evan was exhilarated by Lindy's response to his interest in her. He whistled, sang, and made lots of noise, but with nobody to hear him, soon fell silent. He needed to see her again soon, retrieved Lindy's number, and dialed without hesitation. He had never seized the moment before but vowed to do so now.

Reaching her voicemail, Evan left the following message: "This is Evan Brinkley. I have reason to celebrate and would like you to join me. Please call me at 755-1090 to work out the details." He would never have thought of being so presumptuous until his illness, but now it seemed perfectly natural.

It never occurred to him that Lindy would not return the call, and later the same evening, she did.

"Hello Evan, this is Lindy."

"Hi! How's 7 PM on Saturday?"

"Fine. What are we celebrating?"

"I'll fill you in on Saturday. Dress up."

"Sounds mysterious, but interesting," she added.

"I have your address and know the street. I won't have any trouble finding you."

Laughing at his directness, she said, "Apparently not. Bye."

Evan washed his car, shined his shoes, selected another new shirt to match a new suit, and made reservations at a fine restaurant adjoining Lake Coeur d' Alene. Used to growing increasingly uncomfortable before social occasions, he never considered now that this date would be anything but a success. On the ride to Lindy's, he whistled and sang to the tunes of a 50's station, another first for him.

Lindy lived in one unit of a tastefully appointed, heavily wooded four-plex. He rang the bell, caught her off guard by stealing a kiss, walked in and looked the place over. Evan was not surprised to discover that the rooms were immaculate and well furnished. She had been able to fit the furnishings to the condo complex. The rooms were woodsy, yet bright and cheery. He moved quickly through the condo and then came back to Lindy.

She asked, "Did I pass inspection?

"With flying colors. Are you ready?"

"I'll get my coat. Where are we going?"

"It's a surprise. You'll have to be patient."

"Like you?" she laughed.

He smiled and took her arm. They chatted easily in the car before reaching the fine restaurant he had chosen, The Fruit Bowl. Parking nearby, he steered Lindy across the street and into the restaurant's lobby.

Upon identifying himself, he and Lindy were seated immediately in a comfortable booth. After each ordered a glass of wine, she smiled and said, "All right, I've waited long enough. What are we celebrating?"

"This is my retirement party. I've already done the family number and the fellow employee thing, but now I want to share it with somebody special. You are at the top of the list."

"Congratulations. I'm flattered, but what's so special about me?"

"Nothing in particular, until you smile. Then I want another one and another. Your smiles are addictive."

"Since you put it that way, I have several questions."

"Fire away."

The questioning continued throughout the leisurely dinner. Neither took their eyes off each other, except to manage food. She began probing his childhood and his job, then dug more deeply into his marriage.

"Why do you marry your wife?"

"Because she asked me. It never occurred to me to refuse."

"Why did you have three children?"

"Because she wanted them."

"Do you miss her?"

"No. She dismissed me long ago. I was a convenience, never a partner. When she died, I felt like a visitor at her funeral. Our daughters cried, but I didn't."

"Why are you so assertive now?"

He hesitated before responding, "I'm making up for lost time."

She started to ask another question, but he interrupted by suggesting that they take a walk. Lindy nodded in agreement as he tipped generously. Walking with her was as comfortable this time as last. Her gait was smooth, even when she turned her head to speak to him. Her communication skills were highly developed; Evan especially appreciated being listened to after years of being ignored. As they spoke, his confidence grew. Returning to the car, he admired how gracefully she entered the driver's seat.

"Let's do it again," he said.

"Friday or Saturday?"

"How about both?"

"Let's try Friday and see how it goes," she responded, laughing.

"Friday it is."

CHAPTER IX
SHERI DIGGERS

Though flattered and energized by his budding relationship with Lindy, he remained determined to even old scores. On a long walk the following day, he decided upon his next victim.

Evan worked for Medfast for thirty years. During that time, most of its employees respected Evan's need to be left alone; Sheri Diggers, a successful saleswoman, was an exception and tormented him relentlessly during his thirties. She was a well-proportioned, thrice-divorced brunette with beautiful green eyes, a spell-binding smile, and a mean streak. She was also meticulous about her clothes and grooming.

He did whatever he could to avoid her, but she did not keep a fixed schedule and often surprised him. Sheri would stop at his desk and run her hands through his hair or straighten his tie. On these occasions, Evan blushed deeply. The more embarrassed he became, the more she prolonged these episodes, which had become office events. When word of an impending Sheri-Evan visit was circulated, workers would drop whatever they were doing and secure a vantage point.

One day she went too far. Evan was returning to his desk when Diggers jumped at him from a little alcove, lassoing him with a bright scarf and kissed him on the forehead and each cheek. She was slow in turning him loose, while inspecting her work. She smiled brightly and retracted her scarf, noting the three bright red outlines of her kisses made by the lipstick. Unaware of the lipstick, Evan retreated to his desk and a pile of paper. He failed to notice that the laughter was louder than usual.

As the afternoon wore on, the volume of traffic past his desk increased; some made extra trips to look at Evan. On a restroom trip, he encountered his boss in the hallway.

"Enjoying your break, Brinkley?" needled Mr. Abrams.

Puzzled, Evan continued to the restroom, where a mirror told him all he needed to know. Thus, the legend of "Three Kiss" Brinkley was born; this nickname hounded Evan and refused to die. Now, Sheri must pay.

Evan acknowledged that he made an easy target for people who did not play fair, with Sherri being the best Medfast example. He also knew intuitively that Sherri and others bashed him not simply because they could, but because Evan was a better person, not just smarter but more decent and civilized. Their cruel hazing was fueled by feelings of inferiority and their inability to reach him in any other way.

Sheri had finessed her way into a senior Medfast sales position and took great pride in her presentation skills. The sales staff met on Thursday afternoon, and Sheri always addressed them.

She did not care much how strongly her colleagues resented her as long as she was the center of attention and looked her best.

As long as she was in a game, she would find a way to win; just ask her three ex-husbands, who had been badly overmatched.

By using the company website, Evan verified that the following Thursday was a special day for the sales staff and that Sheri would be giving the keynote speech. After looking through a box of materials that had been left in his garage by a neighbor and former bank officer who had died recently, he found just what was needed. This was almost too easy!

On Wednesday, Evan assembled a package and fedexed it to the Medfast VP for Sales, indicating that it should be presented to Sheri before her speech. Late Thursday morning, Evan entered Medfast's back door and went to an isolated room which had intra-building television access. With little trouble, he was able to receive a signal from the cafeteria annex housing the sales meeting. He made himself comfortable and watched as the sales staff milled around and then took their seats.

Beginning the meeting, the Sales VP dispensed with minor matters and then introduced Sheri. He surprised her by giving Sheri a nicely wrapped package and asking her to open it. She did so with a flourish and then opened the package within a package, immediately spraying paint all over her clothes, in her eyes, and on those around her. The paint pack used to explode with bank money had worked perfectly. Sheri began screaming and swung her arms violently, hitting those who tried to help her. Evan had seen enough and shut down his television access, smiling contentedly as he slipped out the building's rear exit, unnoticed as he had been for many years.

CHAPTER X
MORE LINDY

Lindy was busy during the week; her lack of availability on most weekdays due to extensive travel meshed well with his plans to get even with his former tormentors. On Thursday evening, he called her on her cell phone and asked her to have dinner with him on Saturday. She countered with an offer to prepare dinner for him. He accepted gratefully and asked what he could bring.

"Just your charm and wit."

"I'll have trouble finding a big enough container," he said and then regretted it because he sounded so hokey.

"You'll manage somehow," she laughed and signed off.

The sound of her voice both lifted and inspired him. Evan was already thinking of the most appropriate wine he could bring and what he would wear. He also needed a haircut, but not the ho-hum kind he had been getting for years. Having heard of a good stylist with a shop in a downtown hotel, he called and was able to secure an appointment for the following day. He brought a male model picture from a magazine with the type of hair style he wanted. The stylist thanked him for doing so and came close to duplicating the effect with Evan, who tipped generously.

Evan used the next 24 hours to do household chores. Mary and Cary called and he had brief, lively conversations with each. He selected his shirt and pants without second guessing himself and slipped on a new pair of loafers, shunning his wing tips. Evan was glad that Lindy was waiting for him, but with his newfound confidence, he concluded that if she wasn't, he would be able to find someone else. The old Evan would have felt guilty for feeling that way, but not the new Evan. He smiled at the mirror and headed for his car, making a mental note to look at vehicles next week more suited to his emerging identity, but sadly he would be leasing rather than purchasing.

Stopping to buy a bottle of zinfandel and a single white rose, he pronounced himself fit company. Upon answering the door, Lindy laughed out loud as Evan struck a comic pose. She was ready for his kiss this time and returned it gently but firmly, motioning for him to take off his tasteful shoes, which she noted with approval. He joined her in the kitchen as she finished preparing the meal. Perched on the countertop, Evan had a great view of his charming companion. Though barefoot, she looked taller than her 5' 4" because of her tailored black slacks, lime sweater, and long black hair. Lindy looked good, knew it, but did not flaunt it.

"I should charge you for having too much fun," he observed.

"I couldn't afford it," she responded happily.

Until now, he had avoided asking her about her personal life pre-Evan. At the risk of spoiling a wonderful moment, he inquired, "Why isn't there some guy already in this picture?"

"There was, but he passed. Jeff was a wonderful guy and a brave marine. His loyalty to his fellow marines accounted in part for his death." She looked out the window for a moment before continuing, "He was different than you in many ways, but he was able to make me feel like a better person. You have the same effect on me."

She turned to look at him and there was no doubt that she meant every word. He went to her and held her before she set the pot roast on the table. As they ate, they talked of many things, each taking greater pleasure in listening than speaking. So engrossed were they that both seemed surprised when the food and wine were gone. As though they had been together for years, Lindy and Evan cleared the table and then sat on the couch, holding hands without speaking. After an hour, Evan rose, took Lindy's hand, and walked her to the door. Afraid to break the spell with words, they hugged and kissed, and he left silently. Never before had he felt so alive and appreciated. He walked to his car, dazed and smiling.

CHAPTER XI
ILLNESS

He slept dreamlessly that evening but woke feeling the full effects of his illness for the first time: a slight headache, blurred vision, severe nausea, and weak limbs. He staggered from the bathroom to the kitchen and felt better after having a muffin and orange juice. Evan wandered into his backyard, trying to regain his strength. Gazing into the cloudless sky, he realized how little time he had left and how his rapidly developing relationship with Lindy had complicated his decision-making.

There was at least one more score he had to settle before turning his attention to Lindy. The person involved clearly had hurt Evan the worst, deserved the most severe payback, and presented the most challenging target.

A strapping six-footer, Jerry Burns had been in Evan's high school class, played football, dated widely, and enjoyed the admiration of students and teachers alike. Jerry was everything that Evan was not. In addition to his attributes, he was an inveterate bully, clever enough to wound people emotionally but not sufficiently sensitive to realize the damage he caused.

In his sophomore year, Jerry began making friends with Evan. Though initially suspicious, Evan was so desperate for friends that he overcame his misgivings.

During December of that year, two boys began shoving Evan back and forth in a hallway near the school's cafeteria. Jerry happened along and cracked the boys' heads together. The word soon spread that Evan had a protector; for months, Evan enjoyed free passage in and around the building. He loved being able to go the library and remote areas of the school without fear of bullying. Evan always waved to Jerry in the halls and made it a point to have Jerry see him.

Before mid-terms in March, Jerry stopped Evan in the parking lot and asked for a brief tutoring session. Evan, of course, agreed and the boys went back to Evan's house in Jerry's car. Several students saw them leave and were duly impressed. Jerry's problems with the accounting class were addressed quickly because he was a quick study and because Evan explained things clearly.

Evan's mom and his sister, Cecilia, took to Jerry quickly and asked him to stay for supper. Jerry called home, got permission, and proceeded to charm Evan's family. Cecilia, an eleventh grader, would have been happy to sit in the living room and simply observe Jerry. Jerry, however, insisted on teasing her, and she became flustered, while enjoying the attention immensely.

A few weeks after this visit, Jerry offered Cecilia a ride home from school and she quickly accepted. He surprised her by turning off the direct route to her home and stopping on a road in the middle of a heavily forested area. Jerry explained that he wanted to test her powers of concentration and blindfolded her. He then took off her shoes, while explaining that it was part of the test. As darkness was setting in, he drove off, laughing cruelly. Four hours later, Cecilia arrived in a police car, stunned and frightened. She never fully recovered from this incident, often lapsing into a daze, even in public.

Evan approached Jerry at school to talk about this matter, but Jerry roughly shoved him aside. Jerry never spoke to him again.

While devising a plan, Evan took a walk through his neighborhood. He knew that Jerry had married a wealthy young woman and lived in a nearby town and also that he was having an affair with a single woman, Donna Wilson, who lived within a mile of Jerry's home and traveled extensively as a sales representative. She and Evan's wife were friends and the Brinkleys had been in Donna's nicely appointed apartment on two occasions.

Evan realized that squaring things meant that he was going to have to hurt Jerry badly to atone for the damage done to her psyche and her feet during her long walk. Before visiting Donna on the weekends, Burns would park his flashy, new convertible on a side street a few blocks from Donna's place and walk through an alley to reach her apartment. His usual parking spot was in a sight line with the apartment. He would then ascend a sheltered stairway to the second floor and turn left to her apartment. In front of her door, there were linoleum strips over wooden supports; nails held the strips in place and woodscrews held the supports. Under the doorway, there was a ten-foot drop to a cement walkway.

Noting that her mail box was full, which meant that Donna was traveling this week as usual, he returned home and took out his tool kit. Setting his alarm for 3 AM, Evan went to Donna's apartment and loosened the nails holding the strips and the screws holding the planks and then tightened them again.

After dark on Friday night, Evan waited in the bushes near Donna's apartment for three hours, hoping to see Burns park his car. Since Burns was a no-show, Evan went home at midnight, vowing to be patient. The next evening he returned to the same spot at the same time and soon after arriving saw Jerry park two blocks away. Evan quickly ascended the stairs, removed the nails and screws, and then put the linoleum and boards in place.

He took his spot in the bushes and Burns soon appeared. Moving silently up the stairs, he approached the apartment door and for a time seemed suspended before falling through the loosened strips and boards to the cement below. Evan heard the unmistakable cracking sound of one or more bones breaking and saw him fall backward and hit his head. His work here was done. As he moved down the alley, he could hear apartment doors opening and Burns moaning.

CHAPTER XII
SHARON

Evan had had enough revenge and now vowed to leave his daughters with a clear idea of how he felt and what each meant to him. Evan was determined to make these important people in his life understand that he was a concerned, proud father.

He called Sharon and explained that he wanted to speak with her privately. He arranged to pick her up at 1 PM on Saturday. Evan drove to her home and caught Sarah and Rachel coming out the door. He hugged each child and tousled their hair, before they ran down the block. Sharon appeared in the doorway and he motioned her outside.

"I'll need to get my cell," she said.

"Forget it. You won't need it," he told her.

She hesitated but did as she was told, for the first time in a long while. Evan drove towards his favorite spot on the lake and he and Sharon talked about his grandchildren, her job, and other family matters. As he parked the car, they joined each other on the road and began walking. After Evan gave her his car's GPS information, she began asking more questions, but he surprised her by raising his hand and silencing her.

He began, "When you were born, I was more curious than proud, and more relieved that you were healthy, than happy that you were so pretty. I held you very carefully and you would make soft, cooing sounds. I used to check to see if you were tangled in your blanket or positioned uncomfortably, but I rarely attempted to tease you. You intimidated me with your stare, as if you could look right through me. I was as proud of you then as I am now, but I didn't know how to show how I felt."

Sharon considered his statements and asked, "Was I a difficult baby?"

"Not at all," Evan replied. "You were easy to train, insisted on dressing yourself, and spoke early and well. I used to see other fathers in the park, laughing and joking with their children, but I could never think of anything to tease you about. I was always relieved when I got you home without a fuss. Once, a mother pushed her carriage up to you and her little boy smiled and laughed at you. You joined in and the two of you were having a great time until you looked at me and immediately put on your poker face. I was crushed because I felt that I had ruined your happy time. I always imagined that I was a wet blanket in any situation."

"That really never changed, did it?"

"No," he replied. "If anything, it got worse. When you started toddling, your mother took over."

"When I was in elementary school, I always imagined that you were in a parallel universe, but I was puzzled because there did not seem to be anybody else, not even mom, in your world," Sharon speculated. "My sisters, mom, a few girl friends, and our friendly neighbor, Mrs. Wainscot, were in mine. I worried occasionally because it seemed that my friends and classmates had bigger, richer universes than

I, but then I decided that's just the way it was and accepted it."

They walked in silence, while Evan weighed her comments. "When you were in high school, the barrier became impenetrable. You managed time well and went to your mother with your rare concerns. I don't ever recall you asking me for anything other than teaching you how to drive. I find that interesting because you're still a lousy driver.'"

Sharon started to protest, but then looked at her dad and smiled painfully. She realized that driving was largely a science, but with a dash of art. Sharon had the science down cold but did not always display the flexibility and imagination needed to extricate herself from embarrassing driving situations, such as backing from a parking space.

"When high school boys came around for you, I always treated them and your girl friends with respect," he said.

"I know you did, dad. They didn't quite know what to make of you, but you were not one of those fathers who were reliving their childhoods. For that, I'll be eternally grateful. You never embarrassed me and I could count on you. Because you were predictable and respectable, I gained confidence from that. Don't sell yourself short, dad, just being there and remaining constant was worth more than you know."

"Thanks, Sharon. I'm sorry that I had to get sick to initiate this conversation. What a shame it would have been to pass without hearing those kind words."

They hugged gently and he took her hand before completing their walk, each with eyes brimming with tears. After walking Sharon back to her home, he stopped to chat with Bill.

She stood on the second floor landing and watched the two men in her life, speaking softly and listening to each other intently. Sharon was usually too busy to spend time observing and realized that she had been missing important things. In this case, she noted the strength of these two men, whom the world takes so lightly. From that moment on, Sharon vowed not to treat Bill the way her father had been treated. She would quit taking her husband for granted. As she turned from the railing, Sharon was already planning ways to include him gradually, without alarming him.

CHAPTER XIII
MARY

Evan guessed that he could find Mary at home, but he elected to call, because he did not want to take time away from her school work if she was grading papers or planning. When he did call, he asked if she had an hour for him, and she quickly said that she did, telling him that Ned had just started his nap. Evan hurried over and was soon sitting with Mary in her comfortable living room.

"Is anything wrong, dad?" she asked.

"Just my terminal illness," he responded.

Mary looked stricken and about to cry. Her emotions were always near the surface and subject to immediate change.

"Bad joke," he apologized. "I'm as good as can be expected, but this isn't about me. There are some things that I never got around to saying, and I'd like to say them now."

"OK, dad," she said uneasily.

"By the time we got you home from the hospital, you were the supportive, caring human being you are today. I have always been proud of you. You reached out to people, even as an infant, and have never stopped.

I liked to arrive early to pick you up from pre-school and watch you comfort any child who was crying or was sad. On a playground a few years later, you broke up a fight between two husky boys and got a finger in your eye for your trouble. I wasn't there then, but I was told that the two fighters supported you under each shoulder and took you to the pre-school office. Apparently, the boys felt worse than you did."

"I remember that. My eye was irritated for a long time. I didn't know that you even knew about it," Mary said.

"You always were more concerned about others than yourself. Your little friend Karen used to tease you but you never teased back,"

Evan continued. "If she was sad, you would do anything to make her smile."

"I didn't think you would remember Karen. I had other friends," Mary said.

"But none as nasty as Karen," said Evan, smiling. "When you used to play with your pack of girl friends, I always envied the confidence and unrestrained joy you displayed. I recall your howls of laughter vividly. Any one who could laugh that way had to be a properly centered human being and a person others would want to be around."

"I didn't always laugh, dad. Sometimes I was sad."

"I know, Mary, but you never allowed yourself to be sad before you made sure that everyone else around you was as happy as you could make them. Do you remember when your friend, Cindy, was going through a divorce in her family? You suffered along with her and talked with her for weeks, until you finally convinced Cindy that the split was not her fault. I was so proud of you."

"Why didn't you say something, dad?" she asked.

"It's not my style," Evan replied.

"I thought your silence meant you were unhappy with me," Mary said. "I would have done anything to make you happy. I just didn't know how."

"You have made me happy, more than you will ever know. My belief in a Supreme Being is a little foggy, but I do believe there will be a final weigh-in for every person on a big balance scale. On one side are the ways in which you have harmed others and cheapened yourself, and on the other, the good deeds you have done for others. I believe you will leave this world with your many good deeds far outweighing your few shortcomings.

By contrast, I do not believe I will leave much of either good deeds or shortcomings. I have lived for fifty-one years, will die soon, and will scarcely leave an imprint upon this earth. I have been a spectator, not a participant, in a world in which I never was able to demonstrate passion for anything. It wasn't that I was misunderstood, but rather that people didn't care what I thought or did because I couldn't convince them that I cared."

"How about my teen dates?" Mary asked.

"How about those dates!" Evan responded. Mary was surprised by the quick wit which her father now displayed and she laughed.

"I did reach out to others as I dated, often seeing troubled boys. I tried to fill holes in their lives and it did create some awkward situations. I'm sorry about that."

"Don't be. I knew what you were doing and in my own way, I tried to keep you from getting in too deep. Do you remember when you discovered me sitting outside that wild party? I was uneasy with that spirited boy who stopped by for you that evening. What was his name?"

"Jeffrey Archer. He was a heavy drinker and a brawler. I thought I could bring him around, but I was overmatched. I was glad to go home with you that evening."

"Whatever happened to him?"

"You don't want to know," Mary responded. "I couldn't reform everyone," she laughed.

Evan pleased her by replying, "But I love you for trying. You have built a nice life for yourself and I'm proud of you. I'm sure you're a great teacher. Why don't I leave you to your work now? Thanks for being you."

Mary hugged him impulsively and he hugged back with enthusiasm. Before leaving, Evan looked in on Ned, straightening his blanket and kissing his brow. Evan thought of how much he would miss Ned.

CHAPTER XIV
CARY

The next day, Evan called Cary and made plans to visit her. When he arrived, Cary was listening to her husband, Monte, on his radio station. They sat for a few moments as Monte introduced a hard rock song with a clever anecdote. He was glib and funny.

"He was good before and he's getting better," Evan observed.

"Did you ever tell him that?" Cary asked.

"Don't be so defensive," Evan paused. "You know, I guess you're right. He always seemed to fill whatever room he's in, and I had trouble with that. I'll make it a point to tell him."

"You better make it soon," she answered.

Now it was her turn to be embarrassed. "I didn't mean it that way, dad. What I meant to say was that he had a recent interview with a San Francisco station that he felt went well. We may be leaving Spokane."

"How do you feel about that?"

"Excited and a little threatened," she responded.

"You always liked a challenge," he ventured.

"There was always someone around to pick me up when I stumbled," she said.

"That someone was always your mom, wasn't it?"

"Most of my problems were small. I always felt that if I ran into a serious problem that you would emerge from the shadows and help me.

"Did you really believe that?"

"I still do," she said. "That's why I made it a point to be such a pain, because I could test limits without concern. You were my insurance policy for catastrophes. You were a puzzle, both solid and mysterious."

"I was a puzzle to myself, also. I knew you were frustrated and lashing out, but I supposed that was just part of growing up."

"When I smoked pot and refused to get out of bed for a few days, what did you think of that?"

"I thought that you were confused and would think things out," Evan answered.

"All you had to do was to tell me to straighten up," Cary asserted.

"Your mother did that."

"Yes, but she always was telling me stuff. If you had said something, it would have meant more."

They listened to Monte finish the show smoothly and Cary explained that she and Monte had prepared a demonstration tape, stressing how important that tape was in becoming successful in his profession. Evan asked several thoughtful questions during this discussion, questions which Cary appreciated deeply.

"Dad, you're sick and yet you're still interested in our lives."

"I always have been. I just didn't want to be intrusive."

She responded, "I wish you had intruded more because there were times when I sure could have used you. Perhaps I would have gone directly through school instead of moving sideways for so long."

"Maybe you would have put it in reverse. People need to find their own way."

She paused, "Yes, maybe you're right."

"In any event, now that you are moving forward, why don't I get out of your way so that you can finish your nursing homework? Your mom would have liked you as a nurse and so do I."

"Dad, about you and mom..."

"I simply didn't bring enough to the relationship to make it worth her while."

"Or you didn't try hard enough to sell what you had. Most people are selling a weak product, but not you," she said, hugging him.

CHAPTER XV
WHEN YOU WALK

Rain began as Evan was drifting asleep and continued unabated as he awoke. Ordinarily, this type of storm caused him to withdraw and take cover. Despite the fact that he had spent most of his life retreating from threats, real and perceived, things were different now. After a breakfast of oatmeal and juice and despite a slight fever, he donned his rain gear and left his home, heading directly into the teeth of the storm. Walking purposefully and leaning forward, he dared the storm to slow him or discourage him in any way. He was sweating freely under his attire as the rain bounced wildly off his rain outfit.

Evan fought fatigue desperately, vowing to challenge the headwind. After three miles, he was on the edge of town and at the complete mercy of the elements. When he felt he was fully spent, Evan spied a large mail storage box at least a quarter mile away and willed himself to reach it. As he staggered the last few steps and fell heavily against the large metal container, his breathing was irregular and labored. While resting for five minutes, Evan savored the pride in his accomplishment but knew he still had to make the return trip. With the wind at his back, Evan walked erect and let the wind propel him. Though stumbling several times, he was able to gather himself and return home without incident.

As he pealed off his clothes and entered the shower, he experienced a mixture of weariness and elation. While leaning on the shower wall and adjusting the spray so that the water bounced off him like pellets, Evan reflected upon this walk, clearly a fine physical achievement. He understood now more fully why athletes competed and made extraordinary sacrifices, perhaps to get this very feeling. Was he experiencing the endorphin high? Why had he chosen to be such a fringe player and not participated more fully in life's opportunities? What other things had he missed because of his passive nature? Was he born this way or had he opted out at some point?

He pondered these questions as he completed his shower. Ravenous, he ate two frozen dinners, more food than he had ever eaten at one sitting. In an easy chair, he sorted mail and skimmed the newspaper, while making a mental note to cancel his subscription. He fell into a deep sleep almost immediately and woke two hours later, stiff and weak, to the ringing of the telephone.

"Hello," he managed in a hoarse voice.

"Hi, sunshine. It's Lindy. Are you all right?"

"Just woke up. You surprised me. I thought you were out of town."

"My flight was canceled because of the weather. Do you want to get together?"

"Yes, I'd like to see you. We need to talk."

"Uh, oh! I've heard that one before, and it never turns out well."

"It's not like that. Come over and you'll understand. I'll order Chinese."

"Don't bother. I'll pick up a chicken. I had Chinese yesterday."

"Drive carefully," he said sincerely, but she had already hung up.

Evan gave the house a hasty cleaning after slipping into jeans and a plaid shirt, while planning how to explain himself. He was waiting at the door with a towel as she entered and gently patted her dry. Evan took the package of food into the kitchen and sliced the chicken. Lindy busied herself with the side dishes and they filled their plates. He poured iced tea, and they sat at the table which had served his family for thirty years. She was eager to hear what he had to say, but Lindy curbed her impatience, matching him bite for bite. As they cleared the dishes, he hugged her playfully and she responded indifferently, not making this easy for him. They moved into the living room, and sat facing each other.

"I'm dying," he said.

"Aren't we all?" she quipped.

"No, I only have a few more months to live."

She hesitated and studied him carefully, stating that "You're serious, aren't you? I knew something was wrong, but I didn't realize how wrong. What can I do to help?"

"You've been helping me since the day we met. You are helping me now, just being here."

His eyes were wet with tears and his voice was quavering. Evan desperately wanted her to understand him, and he searched her eyes for some hint of comprehension. Without a sound, she moved to his side of the couch and put her arms around him, hugging him and silencing him by touching his lips when he started to speak. They held each other for a long time before disengaging. Evan followed Lindy to the kitchen table, as she removed a calendar from the wall.

"Schedule me in during the next two months for as much time as you want. I'll be very disappointed if you don't want me around as often as possible," she said firmly.

Her compassion, directness and toughness were exactly the stimulants he needed. In response, Evan improved his posture.

"I'd like a road trip weekend later this month," he suggested.

Without hesitation, she penciled in the following weekend and added a notation on Saturday's date, "Pick you up at 8 AM here."

Evan smiled as Lindy penciled in some other dates per his requests. "That's enough for now," he pronounced.

She looked at him quickly, but he waved off her concern, assuring her that "he was just tired." He walked her to the door, exhausted but happy, kissed Lindy deeply and then locked the door behind her. Staggering, he walked directly to his bed and fell into a heavy sleep.

CHAPTER XVI
CHICAGO TRIP

Evan awoke groggy and gained his feet unsteadily, determined to do something to change his fate, even if it was desperate. He went to an article lying on his coffee table, which summarized research on stomach cancer. Evan learned that University of Illinois-Chicago campus researchers were intrigued by a promising cure: a session with a hyperbaric oxygen chamber followed by a chemical cocktail. The investigation was in the early trial stages; the trials' two components were being tested separately and it will take at least two more years to receive approval for human testing, even if things go well. He had weeks to live, not years, but the new Evan was willing to take a chance.

Through an Internet search, he quickly learned that a hyperbaric chamber could be rented. Two local calls verified that Evan could rent one without medical authorization and that there were more units available than people wanting them throughout the country. The real challenge was going to be getting his hands on the chemical cocktail at UIC-Chicago. The new Evan surmised that university security would not be as stringent as that in military or private research operations and could be compromised.

A quick Internet search identified a Chicago flight later in the afternoon, but the flight was full and the best he could do was to place his name on stand-by. Evan secured a Chicago hotel accommodation near the medical school, but with no university affiliation. He purposefully did not notify any one of his intentions, because he did not want to make them complicit in what was certain to be a serious crime, perhaps a felony.

He stopped at the bank to get $5,000 in cash, packed a bag, and went to the Spokane airport to see if he could get on the flight. Evan went through security checks, feeling guilty traveling for the first time. As soon as the flight was posted, he stepped up and spoke to the tired but polite woman behind the counter, indicating that it was particularly important that he get to Chicago as soon as possible. She had probably heard every story imaginable and was about to dismiss him, but she noticed something in his eyes that gave her pause.

"If I were you, I would try Northwest Airlines," she said softly, trying not be overheard helping a competitor. "They have a non-stop going to Chicago in an hour. The gate is B-12."

He thanked her, went directly to B-12 and was able to book the flight at the Northwest desk. As he settled into his seat, Evan thought of securing this flight as a good omen. He slept during most of the trip and awoke refreshed but hungry. Grabbing the last sandwich of the evening at an airport cafe, he munched and walked to ground transportation.

Splurging for a cab because of the late hour, Evan studied this usually bustling city, now in repose. At the end of the fifteen-mile trip, he paid particular attention to the UIC-Chicago campus as they drove by its northern edge. Evan was pleased with the hotel's location, which was two blocks from the campus. Because he neither wanted to arouse suspicion nor put himself at risk, he decided against a late-night walk through the campus. Instead, he checked into the hotel, put his few items away and began studying the map which he had copied from the Internet.

The sprawling four-story medical research building was located near the center of the campus and had a major entrance, apparently for the public, and a smaller rear entrance next to a loading deck, presumably for employees. He was going to have to gain access to the building in the morning, but he needed at least six hours of sleep. From the article, he had taken the names of the principal investigators, Fuentes and Callahan, and the working title of the project, " A Two-Step Approach to Treating Stomach Cancer;" the rest Evan would have to learn in order to steal the chemicals. Tomorrow figured to be an interesting day.

CHAPTER XVII
GRAND THEFT

Evan ate breakfast early so that he could be around the medical research building as the employees filed in. Wearing a blue button-down shirt, khaki wash pants, and a brown windbreaker with large, zippered inner pockets, he walked a lap around the facility and then opened a newspaper, while leaning against a pillar facing the building. He was reasonably certain that he was not in the sight line of what he recognized as a security camera, which was attached to the wall over the employee entrance. Evan noted that there was a shift change at 8 AM, and that several employees passed through at that time without having to show their identification card; even those showing their card, merely waved it. He also observed that most of the incoming employees at this time appeared to be medical personnel or administrators; seemingly, most custodians and maintenance workers worked the second or third shift.

To gain access, Evan would have to have a card and an "I belong here" attitude. Watching the employees funnel through the checkpoint, he believed he could feign the attitude. Now for the card! He noted that many of the exiting non-medical personnel wore their ID cards clipped to a jacket or sweater, which they carried in one hand. He tried bumping into one of these workers and making a grab for the card, but he snatched all jacket and wound up apologizing profusely to a young, annoyed white male.

Realizing the risks in trying this again, he backed off to wait for a better opportunity. Ten minutes later, a husky black male carrying a jacket with a card attached approached his wife and two pre-school children and tossed his jacket to his young son. As the man kissed his wife, Evan grabbed the card from the jacket without the boy realizing it and turned quickly to disappear into the throng of departing workers. Looking at the identification, he sat on a nearby park bench and tried to figure out how he was going to morph a two-hundred forty pound black male, John Jefferson, into a one-hundred sixty pound white male, Evan Brinkley.

As a teen, Evan had worked a summer job processing laminates, hating the smells but learning enough to smash two cards together and make a convincing forgery. He walked back to his hotel room where he would not be disturbed and using the iron which he borrowed from Housekeeping, pressed a duplicated picture of himself over John Jefferson's face. It was crude but adequate for his purpose.

He bought a Cubs' baseball cap to hide his face partially during his time at the medical center. After eating bacon and eggs at a corner diner, he returned to his room and napped. He then spent a few hours watching TV and shaving, while filing an open order for a hyperbaric chamber rental.

Returning to within two hundred yards of the medical center's employee entrance, he waited a few moments until the entering workers bunched up before joining the crowd.

He waved his card as did the others, and without making eye contact with the two security officers, Evan moved into the building and stepped into an empty office mid-way down a long hallway. He took a building directory off a desk near the door, dropped it into his inner jacket pocket, and found a remote custodian's storage room.

After stowing his jacket behind a locker, he gave a cursory look at the directory, which indicated that Fuentes and Callahan had adjoining third floor offices. Taking a mop and a bucket from the storage room, Evan found a service elevator and took it to the third floor. Avoiding eye contact with passing employees, he drifted casually past the two offices, noting that one of the doctors was in, presumably Dr. Callahan. He traversed the hall twice, and eventually Dr. Callahan emerged and walked aggressively to a large open laboratory, perhaps one hundred yards from his office.

Evan saw him take a seat at the head of a small rectangular table next to a Hispanic male, probably Dr. Fuentes. Four younger staff with lab coats, two men and two women, occupied subordinate positions at the table.

Evan's presence in the hallway would soon become conspicuous, so he returned to the storage room, where he had left his jacket. He killed thirty minutes before returning to peer through the glass at the meeting, which body language suggested would soon be over. He went to the end of the hallway and waited. Ten minutes later, both doctors returned to their offices, while their subordinates remained to work at laboratory benches.

For an hour, Evan kept moving and drifting by the laboratory until the two women exited the lab and walked toward the dining hall at the far end of the third floor. The two men remained in the lab. Since Evan guessed that the women would be more likely than the men to talk shop, he followed, saw where they were going to sit, took a moment to put his mop and bucket out of the way, bought a soft drink, and sat at an adjoining table. The women spoke of their next day's work schedule but not of the chemical cocktail. The two males (interns Evan guessed) on the team joined the women and after some light chatter began to speak of the progress of the project. They talked earnestly for several minutes.

Speaking to the women as he was preparing to leave, one of the males, Jerry, said, "I'll lock up tonight. See you tomorrow."

Evan followed Jerry back to the lab and saw him enter the laboratory, take a magnetized key from under a back lab table, and unlock a refrigerated unit. He counted what appeared at a distance to Evan to be at least five dozen vials, signed an inventory list taped underneath the unit's top, locked the unit, and replaced the key under the table. As he was doing so, Evan slipped into the lab and hid in a small front office. Jerry took one last look, turned out the lights, and exited, permitting Evan the opportunity to take the key, open the unit, take four vials and two needles, leave five one-hundred dollar bills, lock the unit, and replace the key. He pushed the mop bucket back to the storage room, secured the vials in his jacket, and walked towards the exit. As he approached, there was a loud bit of horseplay near the employee exit. Evan took this chance to wave his card at no one in particular and exit casually.

He returned to his hotel room, immediately iced down the vials, and called concerning the hyperbaric chamber, making an appointment in one hour. Evan realized that he was leaving an obvious trail, but since his time was so short, he reasoned that if he succeeded, he would gladly face the consequences, and if not, that it would make no difference. He walked four blocks from the hotel and then hailed a cab to take him to the oxygen chamber office. Paying in cash, he spent thirty minutes in an oxygen-rich environment, made another appointment for the next day, and went back to the hotel to prepare his injection. The new Evan did not flinch when administering the shot, and he sat down and waited for any effects. Feeling none, he went to bed and slept soundly.

The next morning, he dressed, went to breakfast, kept his appointment in the oxygen chamber, returned to his room, and administered a shot. He booked a Friday return flight and followed the same routine for the next two days. When the chemicals were gone, he disposed of the vials and needles in a dumpster behind the hotel. Hoping for a delayed reaction, Evan traveled to the airport by ground transit and waited for his flight. Other than cloudy urine, he had not felt or seen any effects of his self-medication, but did not regret for a minute giving it a try.

Being the aggressor was beginning to suit him. He was disappointed, not defeated, and proud for not succumbing without a fight, as he had done most of his life. As part of his continuing education, Evan learned what he could accomplish with persistence. Before falling asleep on the plane, he decided that upon his return, he would have his Spokane doctor test vital signs and blood for any changes in his condition, which he could not notice himself.

CHAPTER XVIII
MEDICAL FOLLOW-UP

Evan recovered his car at the airport and drove home through deserted streets, then put his car in the garage and dirty laundry in the clothes washer. Though very tired, he thought it best to leave a call for his doctor, indicating that he did not feel well and was going to bed. Evan asked to see the doctor as soon as possible the following day. At 7 AM, Evan was awakened by a call from Dr. Grimes.

"What's the matter?'

"I'm dizzy and have had sharp pains in my stomach," he lied.

The doctor followed with a series of questions and then asked, "Can you meet me at the office in thirty minutes?"

"Yes, I'm on my way."

Dr. Grimes' office was in the back of an often busy shopping center. At this time of morning, however, there were few cars and even fewer people in evidence, and Evan was able to park close to the office. Dr. Grimes followed him inside immediately and waved him into his office, while seizing his blood pressure cuff and locating Evan's file.

"Your blood pressure is 130 over 80, a little high for you but nothing to worry about, and your pulse is 73. Remove your shirt, please, so that I can check your stomach."

Dr. Grimes kneaded Evan's stomach and said, "I see no changes in your condition, but I would like to run another abdominal scan and have you take a blood test. Jennifer, my nurse, will be in shortly and walk you to the laboratory across the parking lot."

Evan nodded and took a seat, mildly disappointed, but he had been pinning his hopes for improvement primarily on the blood test results, anyway. Jennifer arrived and walked Evan to the laboratory. After being tested, he went home and called his daughters and Lindy; since they were all working, he left voice-mail messages for each and then napped soundly.

Waking in a confused state, Evan plodded through household chores and mail, while fielding return phone calls from his daughters. Lindy was traveling and he did not expect her call until later in the evening. Since Dr. Grimes put his blood test on high priority, he anticipated a call before the end of the day.

Shortly after five o'clock, he received a call from Grimes' nurse, who explained there was nothing remarkable about his test, with the exception of a spike in liver enzymes. The nurse sounded concerned, but Evan was not, because he supposed that the shots had stressed his liver. Jennifer requested that Evan come in to be retested on Wednesday, and he reluctantly agreed. Being dismissive might have aroused suspicion, and it did keep the door open for a delayed miracle.

After eating dinner, he sat down to watch the evening news, when Lindy called. She was upbeat and said that her job was going well.

"I'm tired but still looking forward to this weekend. Do you want me to drive?"

Evan hesitated a moment longer than he should have, and she jumped in, saying, "You've forgotten, haven't you?"

Evan was already looking at his calendar and noticed the weekend they had discussed. "I've had some tests run, and I guess I'm distracted. Forgive me. I've been thinking about going away with you, my schedule is clear, and if you don't mind driving..."

"Not at all."

"Still eight o'clock?"

"Eight o'clock it is. It's a three hour drive."

"Are you sure you're up to this?"

"Quite sure. If not now, when?" he laughed.

"Then I'll see you on Saturday," she responded, somewhat shaken.

CHAPTER XIX
LINDY TRIP

Evan went to bed early on Friday night, hoping that if he got up early and took a power walk on Saturday morning, he would be less sluggish when she arrived. This tactic worked perhaps too well, as he greeted Lindy eagerly, loaded his bag in the car, and then fell into a deep sleep before she had driven ten minutes.

"Hey, ball of fire, give me some directions," he heard her say quite loudly two hours later; the volume of her voice suggested that she had said it more than once.

Evan grabbed the Mapquest instructions and directed her into a pleasant resort, woodsy and secluded. He tried moving quickly to show his vigor, but he staggered and slowed down before entering the resort's lobby. Evan got through the check-in without incident, but felt light-headed and queasy. Upon entering the room, he dropped heavily upon the bed, unable to think clearly and afraid to move. Lindy was doing her best to retain her composure, but she was obviously concerned.

"Do you want me to call a doctor?"

"No. If you would care to take a walk while I sleep some more, maybe I can gather myself. Would you mind?"

"Not at all. Call me on my cell if you need me."

Evan awoke an hour later and struggled to get on his feet. He walked slowly through the lobby and onto the hotel's porch, where he found a comfortable swing facing the path leading to the lobby. He settled himself within his bulky sweater and began swinging slowly. The gentle breeze and the deliberate movement had a good effect upon him. When he saw Lindy approaching, he waved as if proud that he was up. She studied him as she came closer and gave him a nice hug. Was it because he looked like he needed a hug or because of her feelings for him? Evan decided that he did not care, at this point.

"Want to eat something?" she asked.

"Just a sandwich. Is that all right?"

"Fine. Let's go."

Lindy turned towards the restaurant and then realized that she was moving too fast for him. At that moment, they stared at each other, realizing that they were operating on different planes and energy levels, a realization that was painful for each of them. If there ever was a chance for a physical relationship, it ended at that moment, when each realized that the balanced tension that makes for a vigorous connection between man and woman was no longer possible for them. Ever the trooper, Lindy helped Evan collect himself and guided him into the restaurant, and after a brief discussion with the greeter, to a remote booth.

"Do you want to go home?" she asked.

"Only if you want to," he replied.

"OK, we'll stay, but if your condition worsens, we need a Plan B."

Evan felt better after eating and accompanied Lindy to the registration desk, where a concerned agent made sure that the resort's food was not at fault, told them that a medical center was only a short distance away, and indicated that hotel transportation was available, if necessary. As they walked away from the desk, Evan pointed to a small movie theater, which had continuous screenings of old films for guests. They sat through the end of *Casa Blanca* and the first hour of *From Here to Eternity*. Though they held hands, the relationship's perspective had unmistakably transitioned from romance to the provision of care.

As he started walking, he was even more unsteady than before but he was determined to be a good companion and to explore the beautiful resort. As she walked with him, Lindy grew increasingly anxious because of his uneven steps and unsteady balance, as Evan tried to stay on his feet. When his condition became erratic, Lindy steered him back to their room. Strangely, the next morning found Evan up and about, coherent and smiling.

They had breakfast without incident and read the Sunday papers while listening to the Sunday news shows. Evan closed his eyes for a brief time but awoke good-humored and focused.

"Are you ready to go home?" she asked.

"Yes, but I can wait if there is something you want to see or do."

"Thank you, but let's go home. I fly out early tomorrow and I have chores to do."

They packed their bags and stopped briefly at the desk to pay the bill, a situation that made Evan uncomfortable because Lindy insisted on paying. They went to the car and stowed their bags, before Evan walked to the front of the car and drank in the magnificent view for two or three minutes. Lindy never said a word, because she realized that he was looking at some things for the last time.

"You know the best part of this view? I had you to share it with," he said, turning to look at her.

She appreciated his words but they took on a different meaning now that their relationship had shifted. Lindy managed a "Thank you" as she fished her car keys out of her purse and drove towards the exit.

CHAPTER XX
GRANDCHILDREN PARTY

Evan called Sharon in a last ditch attempt to convince the grandchildren of the high regard he held for them. He explained that he wanted to have a party, one which they would remember for a long time. Sharon suggested that the party not be held in any of their homes because the setting would play a major part in the effect upon the children, that is, if the event was to be special, the setting itself must be memorable.

"How about Kay's Cove, Dad. It's closed on Tuesdays, but Bill is good friends with Roger Kay, the owner, and helped him get started."

Other than having heard the name, Evan was unfamiliar with Kay's Cove. "Tell me about it, Sharon," he asked.

"It has little rubber floats in a man-made pond. Kids can get in the floats or push them around in the water which is only two feet deep. Among dozens of water toys, there are little guns which shoot ping pong balls. If you want, you could dress up as a bear and fool the kids for a while. It's very informal and only nerve-wracking when it's crowded."

"Can you ask about next Tuesday, from say, three to six?"

"I'll call right now and phone you back."

Sharon returned the call, indicating that everything would be fine for next Tuesday, but that they would have to park across the street, because the parking lot was being paved. Evan indicated he liked the bear costume idea.

"The kids will love it, Dad. How did you happen to think of a party?"

"I've been thinking of lots of things these days," he responded.

Evan prepared for the party by reviewing the family albums and some pictures which had never been included in the albums. He started to sort the pictures but then realized that his daughters and their spouses would have fun doing that task. Before going to the store for candy, soft drinks, and party hats, he placed the albums and photos in his car trunk. Evan had always disliked parties because they exposed him as a social fraud too timid to let himself go in a group. He did not mind preparing for a party as long as he could stay in motion and not have to relate to people; his party anxiety stretched from pin-the-tail-on-the-donkey to adult charades and had gotten progressively worse.

It was time to change that! Evan drove to Kay's Cove and introduced himself to the owner, Roger Kay, explaining that he was "casing the place for the party," and asking if he could pick up the bear outfit on Monday evening

"You can have it now," Roger said. "We won't be using it for a while."

Evan loaded the costume into his trunk and walked back towards the cove, sketching on a pad how best to involve and amuse his grandchildren. He took into account the ages and personalities of the children and the time of day, determined to make this the best party ever, or at least one that they would remember for a long time. He spent the next few days in party planning and practicing his bear moves in front of the dining room mirror. Waking early the morning of the party, Evan racked his brain, trying to think of how many times he had intentionally made another person laugh. While he had been laughed at on numerous occasions, he could not think of many instances where he deliberately caused people to laugh for any reason.

Evan was challenged by the diversity of the four children: Sarah a grown-up fourteen, Rachel a talkative eleven, Ned a highly verbal three, and Josie a guarded six. Cary was Josie's big sister in the Big Brother-Big Sister program and Josie had attended Brinkley family gatherings before. Coming from a home where she had been ignored rather than abused, Josie enjoyed simply being around the older girls; in return, Sarah and Rachel treated her with kindness and patience. Perhaps the closest relationship was between Josie and Ned. Because Ned asked personal questions, Josie originally was uncomfortable with him, but soon became his closest friend, despite the difference in ages. They often would go off to the edge of a family gathering and chat endlessly.

Wearing the bear suit, Evan arrived early, approached each arriving car, and whisked the children into Kay's Cove, teasing them and holding their hands. Through use of a microphone inside the suit, he was able to be heard clearly and to disguise his voice, so that only the adults knew for sure that it was grandpa. Sarah had her suspicions, but soon got caught up in the fun. Though not in the pool because of the costume, Evan was seemingly everywhere else. He mugged with a plastic fish in his mouth and made sure that all of the children received plenty of attention.

By five o'clock his daughters and their spouses had assembled and were impressed by Evan's command of the situation. At five-thirty, he went to the entrance with Bill and met a pizza delivery man who left four boxes.

Evan stepped into the middle of the group and said, "This bear eats better without fur on his head," and removed his bear head so that all could see grandpa.

Although everyone knew that she did not know it was Evan, Josie claimed loudly, "I knew it all the time." Everyone laughed and Josie blushed but grudgingly joined in the laughter.

The pizza did not last long and soon everyone was trooping to the parking lot. Evan was waiting there and hugged everyone good-bye. It was not just the bulky costume, but Evan appeared larger to everyone as they circled around him. He was decidedly in charge, creating a formidable presence that rivaled Sharon's, no small feat.

Ned studied Evan closely and observed seriously, "You seem different;" grandpa, "but I like you better this way."

Everyone patted Ned and messed his hair before moving to the cars; the three-year old had ended things nicely. Evan had put his bear head back on and waved to everyone as they drove off, before returning the bear suit and an envelope with two one-hundred dollar bills in it to Roger Kay. Roger protested and tried to return the money but Evan accepted none of his arguments and went back to his car, tired and happy. Evan had shown them how much he loved them. For the first time in his life, he had thrown a party and it felt good!

CHAPTER XXI
CHILDHOOD

Evan was exhilarated by the party's success and began thinking of his own childhood. His parents were respected members of the community and very proper people, but his mother and father were parents in name only, seeming to take every opportunity to distance themselves from Evan and his sister, Cecilia.

His father, Mason, ran a furniture store in Spokane, and his mother was a librarian in a public library branch near their home. As hard as he tried, Evan could never picture his father without at least one piece of furniture between him and Evan.

He thought his father was most at ease when in the store after hours, but once Evan had stopped by unannounced and found his father slumped on a big couch, weepy and miserable. When Mason noticed Evan, he became angry and stood staring in a hostile manner, causing Evan to flee. Too young to understand the signs of depression, Evan concluded that he had somehow let his father down. When Mason killed himself shortly after Evan graduated from college, Evan felt that a weight had been lifted from him. He was not surprised that Mason's business debts were greater than his assets, and that even their home was heavily mortgaged at the time of his father's death.

When Evan was in elementary school, Mason tried to work Evan into the store's operations, but Evan had neither the muscle to move the furniture nor the will to sell it. It was obvious to all that Evan did not have what it takes to succeed in business. Since his father lived for the store alone, this one-dimensional approach to life allowed no room for Evan.

He never mistreated his son, never really sat down and spoke with him, and just did not have a place for him. Dismissive to a fault, Mason gravitated to people who could help his business thrive. On his part, Evan retreated as far as he could from Brinkley's Booth and became visibly anxious on the rare occasions when circumstances forced him to enter the store.

Mason's wife, Thelma, did what Mason wanted, made sure the meals were on the table, and managed her children's clothes. She did not take them for walks, even when her two were in pre-school, reading one story each evening and tolerating no interruptions or discussion.

Evan thought of his mother in black-and-white only, never in color, and did not cry once when she died suddenly, while he was in college. As a small boy, he once picked a bunch of flowers with riotous colors and handed them to his mother in the kitchen in an attempt to transfer some color to her. She accepted them with a tight smile, placed them in a vase, but put the vase in a remote corner of their living room.

He remembered going to the funeral parlor and seeing her ashen face and grey clothes, disappointed to see that even in parting, she failed to radiate any color. When the mourners were not looking, he placed a little turquoise bracelet on her wrist. This time, she would neither be able to hide his gift nor retreat from life's color. Evan had always been afraid that if she did not have some color, no matter how slight, that he, himself, was doomed to a colorless existence. The bracelet gave him a chance!

He and his sister spent little time together as children; she was two years older, had two or three close friends, and was always too busy for him. Cecilia helped in the store during the annual inventory, but otherwise only went there when obligated. She kept the door to her room closed at all times and Evan did not gain insights from having a sister as many of his friends did.

When Evan was seven, a boy and his sister were slapping him around in a nearby park, and Cecilia happened along. She took each child by the arm, pulled them close, and warned them not to do "this or any thing like it again, or else." Neither child was eager to find out what "or else" meant, so that was the end of Evan's problems with them.

Grateful for her help, Evan went back to their home and began weeding the family garden, one of Cecilia's chores. When Cecilia arrived a short time later, she assessed the situation, took Evan by the arm, and propelled him firmly away from the garden. He turned to say something, but she was already at work; once again, he had provoked a dismissive reaction. Why was he unable to sustain a human connection?

CHAPTER XXII
FRIEND AUGIE

During his childhood, Evan only had two memorable friendships, one with Augie Grant, a small red-haired boy a year younger than he was, and another with Rush Wilcox, a heavy-set boy in his grade, who liked science. Augie lived on the next block and Evan noticed that he often sat on his front porch, seemingly waiting for something to happen. Evan was on his way to the store to pick up a gallon of milk and on a whim asked Augie, who was sitting on his porch, if he wanted to come along.

"Let me check," he replied as he backed into the house.

His mother came out with her arms folded, looking cross and suspicious. "Where do you live?" she demanded.

"Over there," he said, pointing over his shoulder to his house.

"What's your name?"

"Evan Brinkley," he answered in a quavering voice, already sorry that he had stopped.

"Go directly to the store and back. No side trips. Understand?" she said to Evan.

"Yes, Mrs. Grant."

"Augie, what's your phone number?"

"Aw! Mom!"

"Don't you 'Aw, mom' me. Your phone number or you're not going."

"762-0932"

"You call me if there's trouble."

"Yes, mom," he said and was already moving down his front steps and out ahead of Evan, who peeked over his shoulder to see Mrs. Grant standing solidly on the porch, not missing a thing.

"Hey, wait up!" pleaded Evan.

"I'm not waiting because she may change her mind," he snapped at Evan.

"What does she think is going to happen to us?"

"I'm afraid to ask," Augie replied.

The boys talked about little boy issues, such as marbles, TV programs, and boredom. To other boys, this kind of discussion would have been relaxing and interesting, but to these two, it was painful and awkward. Both knew that these issues were what boys their age were expected to talk about, so they each continued trying.

Finally, Augie blurted out, "I'm afraid of my mother."

"Does she hit you?"

"I almost wish she would, but I don't know how to deal with being hated. She's never had any use for me and never will," Augie stated.

"Where's your dad? Does he travel a lot?"

"He took off right after I was born. I've never seen him. It's just me and my mom and she gets meaner all the time."

"Maybe she'll change," Evan suggested, trying to give him some hope."

Augie gave him a you've-got-to-be-kidding look and they walked in silence for several minutes. Evan was wondering whether he could trust this troubled little boy and concluded that there was little harm in doing so, particularly because it seemed that their conversation had helped Augie. Evan had heard the phrase, "getting it off your chest," and thought he might feel better if he discussed his problems. He had also heard the term, misfit, years ago, and felt uncomfortable because he knew it applied all too accurately to him. Maybe getting some problems off his chest would help make him a better fit with the world around him; at least, it was worth a try.

After purchasing a gallon of milk, Evan fell into stride with Augie on the way home. Augie was afraid to talk any more because he did not want to make Evan uncomfortable, while Evan was slow to speak because he was sizing Augie up, not wanting to set the stage for another breach of trust. He had traveled that road too many times but finally decided that he must trust someone. Whom else did he have?

"My mom and dad ignore me. We never go anywhere together. They never even check my school work or grades, and they go days without even looking at me or calling me by name."

"I'd settle for that," Augie ventured.

"But it's creepy. It's as though I don't exist. When I'm ready to get my driver's license, I wonder if my photo will come up blank."

"I know you exist, Evan," Augie said firmly, while turning to look at Evan, who turned beet-red.

Both boys were embarrassed by this moment and walked back to Augie's house in silence.

"Come over some time, Augie."

"I can't, Evan. You would have to come here to spring me."

"OK, if that's what it takes!"

Their friendship lasted for six months; the bond between the boys grew steadily closer, so that they discussed their deepest secrets. One day, they were sitting on the back steps of the Grant home. Augie was explaining that he enjoyed sitting near a girl in his class and looking at her eyes and hair. Evan did not think of girls in that way yet, but he had several questions for Augie. Deep in conversation, the boys did not see Mrs. Grant standing directly behind them.

"You are terrible for talking about girls that way. You're going to hell, Evan Brinkley. Right now, you are going home and not ever coming back here. Augie, you are going in the house and will never play with this evil boy again."

Augie was crushed and went inside in tears, while Evan turned and ran quickly to a remote area of the park and sat with his head between his knees for more than an hour. He finally had a best friend and now he would not be able to enjoy his company again. Knowing that chances of Mrs. Grant relenting were not good, Evan was depressed for weeks and started looking for another friend. He did not merely like having a friend, but he needed one at his age to share the prism through which he viewed the world.

CHAPTER XXIII
FRIEND RUSH

Evan began searching for another friend, taking two long shot chances in approaching boys at school, but only received a loud, "No," from one and derisive laughter from another. He knew he was scraping the bottom of the barrel when he considered approaching Rush Wilcox, a chubby science nerd, but Evan was desperate. Legendary for his show-and-tell presentations, Rush was in Evan's grade but in another class in his school. Other boys in Rush's class were fascinated by his explanations of the array of lizards and insects he brought to school; however, they did not let this fascination stop them from giving him a wedgie made memorable by adding a nasty looking lizard to the mix. Rush's gyrations in trying to fish the angry lizard out of his pants gave birth to the term: Dancing Rush. Since Rush was rarely seen on the streets, Evan decided to call him on the phone.

"Hello, is Rush there?"

"Just a second, I'll get him. Who's calling?"

"Evan Brinkley, Mr. Wilcox."

"You're not going to be mean to him?"

"No sir, I want to play with him, if he's interested."

"Hello, Evan, this is Rush. What do you want?" he asked fearfully.

"I thought maybe you would want to go the library."

Rush hesitated, "I usually go with my mom."

"I know."

Rush hesitated, before asking, "When will I be home?"

"By five o'clock."

"You'll stay with me all the time?"

"Of course. I'll come right over," replied Evan, hanging up before Rush could change his mind.

Though Rush became winded, they walked quickly to the library. Neither boy wanted to run into the many boys who would tease them or perhaps do worse. Upon entering the library, Rush started directly for the science section, but Evan stopped him.

"Let me pick a book for us this time. Next time, it will be your turn."

Rush agreed reluctantly, and Evan walked him into the Fiction annex; Rush looked as though he had entered a foreign land. Evan's choice was limited to books with two or more copies available for check-out. Evan was a John Steinbeck fan, but had not yet read "Travels with Charley," an autobiographical cross-country motor-home odyssey of the 1950's. Each began reading and soon became absorbed.

After some time, Evan nudged Rush and said, "It's quarter to five."

"Let's go."

The boys checked out their books and talked busily on the way back to Rush's house. They agreed that it would be fun to plot the trip on a map.

"We can't do it at my house," Evan explained, "because my mother doesn't like children."

Rush turned quickly to look at Evan, whose expression convinced Rush that he meant every word; Rush was saddened by the full meaning of Evan's statement.

"My house it is. What time?"

"How about one o'clock? I'll bring two magic markers."

Thus began a friendship that lasted eighteen months. Mr. Wilcox encouraged the relationship and became like an uncle to Evan; this nurturing was important to Evan because his male teachers did not have much time for him since he neither demanded attention like some of the male students nor behaved badly like some of the others.

During that time, the boys investigated varied scientific topics, countries, world and civil wars, famous people, and United States presidents. They talked endlessly and were always surprised at how quickly time passed when they were together. Occasionally, they dodged potentially awkward social situations and felt that the potential for danger or embarrassment was well worth the risk. One rainy afternoon outside the library, Danny, a bully of the highest order, threatened to punch Rush.

Hesitating before stepping in front of his friend, Evan challenged the bully, saying, "You'll have to punch me first."

Danny considered doing just that but even as cruel as he was, he understood that there was something quite wrong about punching a scrawny boy willing to take a beating for his friend. Somewhat confused, he stepped aside and let the boys pass.

"You didn't have to do that," Rush laughed with relief, "but I'm sure glad you did."

Still shaking, Evan said, "We got lucky."

Three days later, Evan walked into the Wilcox home where he was always welcome. Generally, Mr. Wilcox greeted him and had a little joke or story. Mrs. Wilcox was in the kitchen as usual, but this time Mr. Wilcox was slumped with his head upon his arms on the dining room table.

"What's wrong, Mr. Wilcox?"

"It's Rush. He's in the hospital."

"What's the matter with him?"

"He has a heart problem."

"When will he be coming home?"

Mr. Wilcox stared at Evan without answering. Finally, Evan took a chair and looked out the window.

"Isn't there anything they can do?"

"No, he inherited the condition from my side of the family, and research so far has been unsuccessful in finding a cure. He's been living on borrowed time for the past few years. We're going to the hospital now and though he's lightly sedated, I'm sure he would want to see you."

"My mother probably will not let me go."

"I'll call her."

Evan dialed the number and handed the phone to Mr. Wilcox, who very calmly explained the situation to Mrs. Brinkley, informing her that he would bring Evan home after the hospital visit. Not giving her any chance to object, he hung up and went to collect his wife for the trip. Evan's mind was whirling as he waited for the Wilcox's to get ready to go to the hospital. Mrs. Wilcox approached Evan, who was standing near the door, and gave him a gentle hug. As he walked to the car, he tried unsuccessfully to remember when someone had last hugged him. Evan sat in the back of their comfortable Ford sedan and imagined how frightened Rush must be.

Evan followed Rush's parents into the room and peaked around them at his friend, who was only half-alert. Rush's color, never the best, varied from gray to green in the artificial hospital lighting. One parent took a position on each side of the bed and held one of Rush's hands, which left Evan standing directly in front of the bed facing the patient. When Rush looked up and saw Evan, he smiled weakly, clearly glad to see his friend; this smile somehow made Evan feel worse. An older doctor stuck his head in the door and waved his hand, signifying five more minutes of visiting time. When his parents stepped aside and waved Evan closer to Rush, Evan touched his friend's right hand and then kicked himself for recoiling slightly.

"I'll bring you any kind of book you want. Just name it," said Evan.

In response, Rush gave him the same look his father had given him, without speaking. As he turned to leave, Evan's eyes filled with tears. At the door, he hazarded a look over his shoulder and saw his brave friend giving Evan the best smile he had left and flashed him a peace sign, something they had done often as their secret gesture of friendship.

Rush went into a coma that night and died the following Saturday. Mr. Wilcox invited Evan to a ceremony for Rush with a thirty or so friends and neighbors. Surprisingly, Mrs. Wilcox hosted the service and did quite well, speaking firmly despite her tears. After her husband spoke of the love he had for his son, Mr. Landis, a biology teacher, spoke of Rush's deep understanding and respect for science. Mrs. Wilcox then surprised Evan by asking politely if he had anything to say.

Evan reflected a moment and then looked at a large picture of Evan which Mr. Wilcox had placed in the corner of their front room. His first impulse was to refuse to speak, but that would be disrespectful to Rush. Too intimidated to look into the eyes of the other mourners, he directed his remarks towards the picture.

"Rush had two good parents. He was loved and knew it. He told me more than once that his parents taught him how to think things through and how comfortable and warm his parents made him feel.

Rush was my only friend. If he's the last friend I ever have, I still will have gotten the best of the friendship business. He was always kind to others, even when they didn't deserve it. He was the smartest kid I know, but he never made fun of anyone or talked down to them.

When bad stuff happened, he always thought it might be his fault. Rush helped me look for good in a world that was hard on both of us.

We didn't have to talk to enjoy each other's company because we often knew each other's thoughts. I miss him already!" he concluded.

Evan looked at Mr. Wilcox, who smiled, walked to him, and put his hand on his shoulder, stating "he was happiest when he was with you."

The group disassembled slowly and Mr. Wilcox walked Evan home.

Before entering the house, Mr. Wilcox turned to Evan and shook hands, saying "Come over any time if you want to talk, Evan. Having you around made Rush's passing easier for us to handle. Thank you."

Mr. Wilcox walked into the house with Evan and entered the kitchen to speak with Evan's mom. Evan could not remember anyone else other than Jerry Burns and sales or service people being in his house.

"Thank you for letting Evan help us through this difficult time, Mrs. Brinkley. We are grateful that Rush had such a good friend. You must be very proud of Evan."

He then stepped forward and shook hands with Mrs. Brinkley and Evan. Before Mrs. Brinkley could reply, he turned and left. Evan went to his room and did not sleep well for several nights.

CHAPTER XXIV
CHURCH

The pain was with him most of the time now and sleeping was becoming increasingly difficult; he often punctuated his sleepless nights with analyses of his life. Evan had frequent flashbacks of Augie and Rush and occasionally reflected upon his religious experiences.

Evan was a lackluster Lutheran, attending church regularly but believing unevenly. As a child, he was disturbed by the reverend's graphic description of those who were lukewarm and would be spat from God's mouth. He viewed himself as a poster boy for lukewarm activity, being unable to get upset by Christianity's inconsistencies or inspired by its beauty. When inside the church building itself, Evan squirmed and daydreamed from early childhood to the present.

As an eight-year old, he and his sister accompanied their parents to the baptism ceremony of a neighbor's baby. For some reason, the service was delayed and there was an hour to kill. As usual, Cecilia shed Evan and went off with a friend, leaving her brother to wander the sprawling church alone. Hearing muffled laughter, he opened a storeroom door and found himself staring at a teen-age boy and girl kissing and hugging. Seconds later, Pastor Sanborn appeared and asked for an explanation.

The male teen said, "We were praying and this little guy starting making fun of us, Pastor Sanborn."

Evan was stunned by this lie. His inability to respond prompted the cleric to conclude that the allegation was true and to say, "We'll see what your parents have to say about this, Evan."

Evan was terrified, because the worst thing that could happen to his parents was to be embarrassed. He would never forget their smoldering silence on the ride home, a stillness which continued for several weeks.

The most painful church activity for Evan was the annual picnic, which began immediately after a ten o'clock service on the first Sunday in May and did not end until dark. He was desperate to fill the hours with meaningful activities, since he had no playmates. Evan did not seriously consider playing in the softball game, because he was clumsy and became flustered. He would have walked on hot coals before getting on the dance floor or sharing a potato sack in the three-legged race. He did, however, enjoy competing in the chess tournament one year, but after winning twice, a burly kid whispered convincingly to him that if Evan beat him in chess, that he would give Evan a "real beating." The best church picnic for him was the year that the event was shortened by a violent storm.

Though not impressed by the rituals, Evan did try to learn from the messages contained in the Bible and became proficient at turning the other cheek. For solace, Evan looked for alternatives to church.

He believed, for example, that his nature walks brought him closer to God than kneeling in a stuffy church. Observing the behavior of small animals and the beauty of flowers and trees had a calming effect upon him, which elevated him above pettiness and greed. He was fascinated by the beneficial impact of rains, even when punctuated by destructive lightning strikes. Evan learned the names of the bushes and trees in his yard and applied the appropriate fertilizer applications in the proper doses at the correct time of year. He had a respect for nature that he did not hold for his church.

After Evan's wife died, Pastor Sanborn tried to insinuate himself into the family rituals, but neither Evan nor his daughters had any enthusiasm for adopting the pretense of the Brinkley clan being a deeply religious family. Therefore, Pastor Sanborn was not invited to June's service, which was held in Evan's home. Sharon Brinkley handled the cremation, and Mary and Cary managed the children and food. Because of weather problems, June's family's flight was canceled, much to Evan's relief. In a brief conversation with June's sister, he promised to send her pictures of the ceremony and a copy of the obituary from the local paper.

Besides the Brinkley family, seven Brinkley neighbors and four of June's co-workers attended the brief ceremony conducted by Sharon. She recognized each adult guest by name and gave them a chance to speak; all comments were positive and made reference to June's strong personality. His daughters spoke briefly about their efficient, loving, and capable mother and then looked anxiously at their father, knowing all too well that the Brinkley marriage was devoid of sparkle and passion.

"June was a formidable woman," Evan began. "She could do three or more things at once and all of them well. If you didn't get to know her as well as you would have liked, it was because she was in perpetual motion. My three daughters and I owe her a great deal."

The three Brinkley women all breathed easier when their dad quit while he was ahead. They knew that what he said was accurate as far as he went and that if he had tried lying, Evan would have failed to convince anyone.

After the guests left, Evan, his daughters and their spouses, and the grandchildren drove to a nearby lake to dispose of June's ashes.

When Mary and Cary cast the ashes into the lake, all were quiet, except for Sarah, who said clearly and firmly, "Good-bye, Grandma!" The words carried well across the large lake and were so perfectly timed, that nobody else dared to speak as they returned to their cars.

CHAPTER XXV
GRANDPARENTS

On another sleepless night, Evan reviewed memories of his grandparents, who were always kind to him. Though bothered by diabetes, Evan's grandmother, Charlotte, used to tousle his hair and smile at him through her pain. She routinely asked him about his school work and listened carefully to his answers.

She was a pleasant woman, who wore big glasses, bulky sweaters, and corrective shoes. Since they usually visited her late in the day and because she always sat in the same chair, the lingering twilight would cast a halo around her full head of gray hair. In part because of the halo, Evan was awestruck in the presence of his grandmother and felt that part of her had already gone to heaven. When she died, he was not upset because he knew that she would not suffer any longer and he also believed that, in some way, she already had a stake in whatever waited on the other side.

The burial service for Evan's grandmother was a somber affair. Her few surviving friends had their own medical problems and his parents could frown their way through a carnival, so a burial service was a piece of cake. Evan studied his grandmother carefully as she lay in the coffin, still seeing the halo in his mind and continuing to sense an ethereal dimension in this sweet person.

His curiosity increased as he observed the plans for her burial, worrying that placing her in the ground would make her trip to heaven difficult. He continued to study her face for signs of anxiety or fear, but the casket was closed without any changes in her expression. The casket's closing triggered a latent claustrophobic reaction in Evan, causing him to sleep even more fitfully. A few days later, Evan checked out a library book on cremation and decided that this was a suitable alternative when it was his time.

His grandfather, Leo, was a small man with great energy, who used to look deeply into Evan's eyes and seemed to understand how difficult life was for his grandson. Evan was pleased by Leo's visits, which increased after grandma's death. Leo always had something in print form and asked Evan on every occasion to call a few days later and relate "what he knew now" as a result of reading what Leo had left with him. Evan used to prepare his remarks carefully on a yellow pad before making these calls. His grandfather was doing everything possible to bring Evan out of his shell. Though unsuccessful in doing that, Evan did learn to organize his thoughts and to communicate in writing, both helpful skills.

At the time his grandfather died suddenly, Evan was waiting to talk with him about a computer magazine his grandfather had left for him. Evan prepared his remarks carefully on two yellow sheets and tucked them under the cushion in his grandfather's coffin.

Since his grandparents had treated others so well, he assumed that they would receive favorable handling in the hereafter. Evan supposed, as unlikely as it seemed at that moment, that a woman might want to marry him some day and that Evan would become a father. Although he would miss his grandparents' company, he tried to look at their passing as the end of a life cycle. This perspective lent dignity and logic to their deaths.

CHAPTER XXVI
PHILOSOPHY

Evan realized that he was a man without a mission, as though a cork at sea. He let others define him; consequently, his chances for self-satisfaction were slim. While getting on a school bus at the end of a fifth grade day, he was distracted by a scuffle and stopped to watch, blocking the door.

A high-voltage science teacher yelled at him, "Do something, Brinkley, even if it's wrong!"

He was embarrassed by this order, partially because the other kids laughed but also because the teacher had so perfectly summarized the life dilemma in which Evan found himself. He was afraid to make errors, take a chance, or assert himself.

Living in this posture, laughs were few and far between, and Evan had come to realize that life without humor was no fun and had little meaning. He knew children, many of them poor and with no great prospects in life, who laughed all the time and were great fun to be around because they saw themselves in charge of their lives and were willing to risk failure. They sparred with others and tested themselves frequently. Others, but not Evan, could laugh at themselves when unsuccessful, thereby conditioning themselves to enjoy life's victories fully and to suffer life's defeats gracefully.

Evan found it interesting that while he had lived a shadowy, fringe existence with no real energy or passion, he now wanted to examine every conceivable aspect of his life before he exited. In some astonishing way, because his end was near, his life had taken on greater importance and the true value of those around him had become apparent.

Evan wondered how many people like him floated through life stuck in neutral, blaming external forces for their inability to kick life into gear. Because most people do not know how or when they will die, he surmised that many people like him passed feeling cheated and desperately wanting more time. How Evan envied pro-active people and pitied re-active people like himself, who waited for things to happen to them!

Starting in his early years, he justified his re-active nature by concluding that not everyone could be a leader and that followers were also necessary for the functioning of our social order. By swallowing this premise hook, line, and sinker, Evan thereby programmed himself for failure, or at best limited success, as a teacher, parent, and employee. He routinely avoided the many roles, big and small, available for leadership, such as committee chair, captain, and strong parent, which allowed so many people to move back and forth smoothly between leader and follower. Such movement enriched life and made many successful because they were viewed by others as well adjusted. Evan became more entrenched in re-active mode as the years wore on; the emotional and social distance between him and those around him widened steadily.

Since he had received his bad news, he had become increasingly energized and involved in life. It was as though a switch had been turned on and power began flowing. Evan could now see how he had not only shortchanged himself but those around him. Lindy had seen him only at his best, but his children, grandchildren, and fellow employees had now seen both sides. Evan was increasingly pleased by the satisfaction he received in defining himself, making decisions, and setting priorities. There was no doubt in his mind that late, even really late, was better than never.

CHAPTER XXVII
GRAMMAR SCHOOL GIRLS

In a world where the tension between females and males propels the two groups, Evan was at a decided disadvantage. He realized that the payoff went to those who had the ability to confront, combat, and control. Rather than possessing a Triple-C personality, he was beset with Triple-T: timid, tentative, and testosterone-deficient. Being a deep-seated Triple-T limited his options and doomed him to be an eternal passenger, never a conductor. While he analyzed, most of his male peers engaged.

His schoolmates played recklessly on the playground, while working off aggression and developing social and physical skills. An increasing number of girls approached play in the same fashion, not caring that, by so doing, they heightened the gender tension.

A serious test of nerve and courage for second graders was the monkey bars apparatus. One day, Evan watched nervously as most boys and many girls negotiated the metal latticework with little effort, despite the fact that it took considerable upper body strength and rhythm to do so. When the end-of-recess buzzer sounded, Evan turned with the other students towards the school's entrance.

Martha, a big, athletic girl, blocked Evan's path and tested him, saying, "I didn't see you up there, Evan. It's your turn."

"I don't know," he responded nervously.

A few of the other students stopped and became interested in how this drama would unfold. To this day, Evan is not sure why Martha said what she did, but he knew that there was no backing out of this challenge.

He stepped awkwardly up four rungs of the vertical ladder, grabbed the first overhead bar tentatively, and propelled himself slowly across the first five bars. Evan was unaware that Martha had begun her trip behind him across the bars.

When she passed him, he became distracted and fell heavily to the ground. To make matters worse, Martha dropped gracefully from the bars, helped him to his feet, and walked him to their classroom, while supporting him under one shoulder. She deposited him carefully in his seat and casually took her seat across the room.

Because of her composure and athleticism, no one dared to tease Martha about this incident, but Evan was taunted for months. He was unable to respond immediately when the teacher asked him what had happened, but one wag quickly interjected, observing that "His body took a bad hop." Thus, the nickname of Bad Hop Brinkley was born; most never even knew his first name.

In the incident's aftermath, Evan hoped that he at least might have made a friend in Martha, but when he next saw her, she ignored him completely, as though the incident had never happened. He would much rather have irritated her than count for nothing. Evan had been crushed physically and socially, and now emotionally.

In sixth grade, he noticed that some of the girls in his class began maturing physically, were interested in older boys, and ignored Evan and other slower maturing males. Even the slower maturing girls were taller and older looking than Evan. Their jokes about Evan and the other little boys in his class were often cruel, even if the boys did not understand their full meaning. What troubled Evan in particular was that he believed that most of these other little boys would soon catch up physically, socially, and emotionally with the girls in his class, while he would only approximate the girls in size and strength.

In addition, he just did not have the "shock absorbers" necessary to engage in the give-and-take required to toughen him. Most of his male classmates had situational problems that time would soon resolve, but he had a strong suspicion that his problems were chronic. There was nothing in his school's curriculum or his parents' subset of skills that could help children like him, and so, for lack of a jump-start, Evan languished.

CHAPTER XXVIII
HIGH SCHOOL GIRLS

In high school, Evan skipped all of the dances until he was a senior. No girls expressed an interest in him and though he admired many for their beauty, he just did not connect. Evan was told by a big football player that things would be easier for Evan if "he could get his mojo working." Since Evan had no clue what a mojo was and nobody to explain it to him, Evan figured that chances of getting his mojo working were not good.

In mid-April of his senior year, Evan was preparing to skip his prom, keeping his dance attendance perfect. Johnnie Douglas, a bony, auburn-haired free spirit headed for Dartmouth the following fall, changed that by approaching him with an offer that got his attention. Evan did not know Johnnie well, but at the time, Evan did not know anyone well.

Johnnie had been dating one of the identical Benson twins, Holly, and told Evan that Polly, her sister, did not have a prom date and expressed interest in going with Evan, who was flattered by her interest. He had been in a history class with Polly and Evan wracked his brain trying to remember the sound of her voice. He asked Johnnie about her voice and Johnnie conceded that she was quiet but asked Evan to call her. Evan promised that he would.

"Hello, this is Evan Brinkley. Is Polly home?"

"This is Polly," she said in a tiny but pleasant voice.

Evan had written down what he was going to say and he proceeded to his first question, asking, "Do you know who I am?"

"Yes."

"Do you have a date for the prom?"

"No," she replied.

"Do you want to go with me?"

"I think so."

"We could double with Johnnie and Holly."

"All right. I'm sure my parents would want to meet you before the prom. Could you come over on Friday?" she said.

"Yes, I'll be there at seven, if that's OK."

"OK."

So in less than a minute he had made a date for the prom. Now what would he do? His anxiety level was high, but first he needed to get through Friday's inquisition, without using a list as he had done on the phone call. Unless he could think of a tactic, her parents were going to see him sweat and squirm in front of their daughter, whom he scarcely knew.

He called Johnnie and told him that he was taking Polly to the prom. Evan discovered that Johnnie had a date with Holly on Friday night and Evan explained that he wanted all four of them to meet at the same time and that he then wanted to talk to Polly by himself. Evan reasoned that if he had sufficient cover, he could get through the parent interview and get to know Polly and what she expected from the prom evening.

When Johnnie drove Evan to the Benson home, Evan had a chance to study the twins who were waiting on the porch. The girls were five feet, two inches tall, no more than one hundred-ten pounds, and had medium length brown hair. One wore a soft yellow summer dress and the other a white tennis outfit, as though ready for a match. Each had dark brown eyes and looked comfortable with each other, but their posture changed as their attention shifted to Evan when he got out of the car. Wearing a nerdy blue button-down shirt and starchy wash pants, he walked stiffly up the steps.

"Hi, I'm Evan Brinkley," he announced to the twin in the tennis outfit.

"Hello, I'm Holly and not your date," she said in a pleasant manner.

He turned to the other, who informed him, "I'm Polly and I'm your date.

Enjoying Evan's discomfort momentarily, Johnnie remained at the bottom of the stairs, finally bounding up the stairs and steering Holly inside.

"Can we take a walk, Polly? I'll meet your parents when we get back," Evan pleaded.

"OK."

Sneaking looks at each other, they walked to the corner without talking, and in unison, they turned and began to speak. They laughed and fell silent again as they continued around the block. Polly told Evan that she knew his sister and that she had no brothers and only the one sister, Holly. She congratulated him on making the school's honor society and he learned that she also had been selected. The walk was going well, so they took another lap around the block.

"Ready to meet my parents?"

"OK. Anything I should know?"

"They like jokes and probably will tease you. Can you take it?"

"We'll see," Evan replied, somewhat unsteadily.

They entered the house and joined her parents in the front room. After shaking Mr. Benson's hand with his moist palm and nodding at Mrs. Benson, he took a seat next to Polly on the couch.

"I have a question," said Mr. Benson. "What branch of the service were you in?"

"Carl, give the boy a break," interrupted Mrs. Benson. "I'll ask an easy one: Do you own a toothbrush?"

Polly exploded, "Straighten up you two or this discussion is over!"

"We'll behave. On prom night, Evan, we expect a phone call at midnight and both girls home by 2 AM," said Mrs. Benson, instantly all business and very much the responsible parent. "Evan, I plan to give your mother a courtesy call this week. Carl. Anything else?"

"We plan on taking some pictures and we will have copies made for your parents."

"Thank you, Mr. Benson," said Evan, although he could not imagine his parents being at all interested.

From Evan's standpoint, the prom went well. He looked presentable in a tuxedo and combed his hair in a suitable style. The thing he feared most turned out to be the easiest: dancing. Evan let Polly lead and even tried taking the lead himself towards the end of the evening. Polly was graceful, patient, and kind, and he responded by smiling a few times and being attentive without hovering.

Evan assumed that the bullies who picked on him would continue to do so at the prom, but this was not the case. Whether it was the formal attire, their dates, or the loud orchestra, not one nasty word was directed towards Evan.

The midnight supper was also noteworthy. When the twins and Johnnie went to the restaurant rest rooms, Evan positioned himself so that he could see how two elderly diners used their silverware, and then was able to prompt the other three when they came back to the table.

At the Benson's front door, Polly anticipated an awkward moment, since Holly and Johnnie were locked in a lengthy clinch. She reached for Evan, kissed him briefly, and then thanked him. Evan smiled and went back to the car to wait for Johnnie. He was relieved that it was over and satisfied that he had given a good account of himself.

He called Polly on the following Thursday and asked her to a movie. Evan knew that the lengthy pause after his request was not a good sign. She again thanked him for taking her to the prom but explained she had been dating a college freshman who was due back in town over the weekend.

"Good-bye, Polly," was the best he could manage.

"Good-bye, Evan."

He had been used but had benefited from it. Evan had proven himself able to handle a complicated social situation without losing his composure or embarrassing himself and others. He was honest with himself and knew that Polly had made things easy for him; consequently, he would never be quite sure how much of the evening's success was his own. Evan caught himself overanalyzing things again. He decided to accept the prom for what it was: a pleasant evening with a nice girl, nothing more and nothing less. Maybe there was hope for him!

CHAPTER XXIX
ACADEMICS

Evan liked everything about learning: smelling new books, applying math formulas, anticipating the author while moving through a well written piece of fiction, completing answer sheets on standardized tests, and listening carefully to a good teacher explain a complicated topic. He had read once that it was important for people to stretch their minds; he hoped that this was true, because he enjoyed stretching his mind more than anything else.

With only a short time left, Evan found himself thinking about his school years and realizing how strongly a child's school experience defines him for life. Evan thought of learning as his Super Bowl. He had great respect for the game, learning, but much less so for the stadium venues, such as schools and libraries, because the managers of public schools and libraries had to admit everyone. Lowest on Evan's hierarchy were those who showed their disrespect for learning by doing the following: blowing off tests, defacing books, interfering with the learning process, and insulting teachers and students.

His fifth grade teacher, Mr. Preston, encouraged Evan at every opportunity. In his early thirties, Preston was chubby, wore ill-fitting clothes and had ferociously bad breath. Evan did not know or care what "gay" meant, so he ignored rumors that Mr. Preston was gay. What he did know is that each day, he could count on this teacher treating him with respect and encouraging him to learn. Evan did not have many weapons in his fight against loneliness, but he did have a potent one in Mr. Preston.

One Saturday, Evan saw Mr. Preston carrying packages downtown and walking toward a residential neighborhood. On a whim, Evan trailed along two hundred yards behind and watched him enter a six-floor apartment building. After waiting several minutes, Evan entered the lobby and inspected the print roster of tenants available on the wall closest to the elevator. While he observed that most apartments listed two or more tenants, Apartment 324 listed only, "Preston, Jerome."

Leaving the lobby, he walked along a four-foot fence to the back of the building and found a swimming pool and parking garage. Afraid of being discovered, Evan went home but returned often over the next two months to study how Mr. Preston lived his life.

He found out that Mr. Preston led a solitary existence, exclusively so from Evan's observations, and did not even have a pet. His teacher visited a branch library, grocery store, and a Catholic Church, but Evan never once observed him speaking to anyone on personal business. What he discovered worried Evan because he knew that he and Mr. Preston were quite alike.

His teacher's loneliness was apparent to everyone through his posture, tone of voice, and unwillingness to confront classroom problems. Evan realized the importance of changing the direction of his life to avoid becoming a Mr.

Preston. As difficult as the challenge seemed to him, Evan became determined to find some way to inject people into his life and keep them there.

Another influential teacher in his life was Mrs. Hammond in sophomore English, a slim, stylish woman in her early forties, who wore striking clothes and had a piercing stare which stopped everyone in their tracks, child and adult alike. Vaulting her into legendary status, she had once noticed a popular football player defacing a library book and fixed her intent look upon him, until the student pleaded with her, "Please, Mrs. Hammond, don't look at me any more. I'll confess to anything."

Towards the end of class one day in October, Mrs. Hammond said, "Evan, see me after class."

As he approached her desk after class, she was writing on the board.

"You wanted to see me, Mrs. Hammond?"

She turned and fixed her stare upon him before speaking, and he could feel his body shrinking and his posture drooping. Evan wondered how she did that with her eyes alone and desperately tried to think of what he had done wrong.

"I want to talk with you about your theme. You wrote an interesting paper about the works of Nathaniel Hawthorne," she stopped and inspected him.

Thinking she suspected plagiarism, Evan blurted, "I didn't copy it from anyone..."

"I know. I know, Evan. Your paper was just fine, but it could have been even better. I am going to do something I don't ordinarily do. I have a proposition for you: Take this book analyzing Hawthorne's works, read it, and rewrite your paper including some of what you read in this book. I'll grade both papers and enter the highest grade. Are you up to the challenge?"

Part of the Hammond mystique was that no one had ever denied her a request for anything. Returning her stare as best he could, Evan agreed to turn in another paper, while realizing that perhaps she had just given him the biggest compliment of which she was capable, loaning him a book. After school, Evan wrapped the book in his jacket and carried it home. When he read the book, he used new gloves and when he needed to mark a section, he used paper strips between the pages.

Taking short walks when getting stale, Evan spent most of his weekend working on the paper. He understood why Mrs. Hammond had him read her source; it filled in gaps and strengthened his arguments. His new and improved version clearly outshone the original, in large part because Mrs. Hammond's book gave the original a strong boost and also because Evan responded to someone giving him attention and respect.

He arrived at her classroom before she did on Monday morning, so he waited impatiently. She arrived like someone from a stage production, twirling off her coat and dropping her books and purse on the desk with a flourish.

"Good morning, Evan."

"Good morning, Mrs. Hammond."

"Have something for me?"

He had carefully practiced his little speech. Handing her the carefully wrapped loaner book and the old and new themes, he said, "I have three things for you. By reading the book you gave me, I believe I've improved my original theme. Thank you for the opportunity."

She took the book without checking its condition and put it and the two themes in a side drawer.

Before leaving, he observed, "You didn't inspect your book to see if I damaged it."

Fixing him with the Hammond stare, she responded, "If I had given it to most other students, I would have checked. In your case, I don't have to, Evan, because you treasure books as I do. Now, if you'll excuse me?"

In a single assignment, she had complemented, challenged, taught, and humbled him. In the bargain, she had treated him as a responsible adult; he liked the feeling. Although a little off-balance after speaking with her, he realized that she was a formidable person who had that effect on many people. Originally expecting to be flattered for taking good care of her book, Evan now realized that taking good care of someone else's possessions should not necessarily elicit praise, because it was one of many things routinely expected of responsible people.

CHAPTER XXX
DRIVING

On another night when discomfort thwarted sleep, Evan reviewed his driving career. He had learned to live trailing his peers emotionally and socially but felt he must keep up in as many other respects as possible. His parents had remarked that they did not believe that Evan should drive until he was on his own, but nonetheless he registered for a driver's education class, perhaps the first time he dared to cross his parents.

The fifteen-member class was scheduled to meet from 9 AM to 12 PM, Monday through Thursday, for six weeks during the summer. Mr. Bergio, a burned-out math teacher, always taught the class, a combination of classroom instruction and behind-the-wheel practice. The teacher informed him that he would have to have a learner's permit on the first day of class; most of the other students already had theirs and had been practicing with their parents. Evan went in to the Department of Motor Vehicles and secured the learner's permit without difficulty.

Now came the hard part, asking his father to teach him how to drive. One evening, his dad came home late as usual and sat in the living room reading the newspaper. Evan stewed for fifteen minutes and finally worked up the courage to approach him.

"Dad, do you have a minute?"

"What is it, Evan?" replied Mr. Brinkley, without taking his eyes off the paper.

"I need your help in learning to drive," Evan announced.

"You know how I feel about young people and cars."

"I know, but it would be easier if I learned now."

There was something desperate about Evan's request that prompted Mr. Brinkley to say, "I don't have the time, but Josh may have some time."

Leave it to his father to outsource his parenting responsibilities. Evan knew the store's newest employee, Josh Thomas, a recently hired twenty year-old maintenance man, who worked from 9 PM to 5 AM, cleaning and assembling. Evan's father had gone to the store at 4 AM one night during Josh's first week to check on him and found Josh busily engaged in his chores. Mr. Brinkley had spoken favorably of Josh, indicating that he only had to be told how to do something once and that he was willing to do more than the job required.

"Should I call him?" asked Evan.

"No, I'll talk with him. Go to the store at 9 PM tomorrow and you two can work out the details."

Evan rode his lighted bike to the store the next evening, knocking on the back door shortly after nine. Josh opened the door with a smile and they sat on one of at least fifty couches scattered throughout the sprawling store.

"I talked with your dad."

"I hate to be a bother."

"Don't worry about it. Driving is easy and fun," said Josh, and that's the way it was.

He proved to be a good teacher, patient and thorough. They worked together each evening for one hour, and then Evan went home so that Josh could do his job. On the few occasions when Evan struggled, Josh laughed, but it was not mean laughter and Evan would join in. This relationship was what he imagined having a big brother would be like. Driving Josh's old but well cared for Chevrolet, he practiced driving on the store's parking lot and backing into stalls near the loading dock for two weeks before driving through the deserted streets near the store.

After working together for a month, Josh told him, "I can't teach you anything else. You need to drive on highways and in rush hour with someone else. I don't feel that I can assume that much responsibility."

Evan was sad to see this relationship end, but he knew Josh was right. "Thanks for your help," said Evan sincerely, shaking Josh's hand.

Evan went home and found his dad watching television. Since the store was closed on

Sundays, Evan asked his dad if they could take the car out the following Sunday and Mr. Brinkley gruffly agreed to a 3 PM session. Evan wondered if his father would shirk this responsibility, but on Sunday shortly after 3 PM, Evan was backing out of the driveway with his father.

Mr. Brinkley was surprised by his son's skills as Evan worked his way through moderately heavy Sunday traffic. As potential problems arose, Evan remembered directions that Josh had given him and he executed them flawlessly. Josh pulled the car into the garage, took the key from the ignition, and handed it to his father, who said nothing as he went into the house. It was a good thing that Mrs. Hammond had taught him that responsible behavior is expected and often goes unrewarded or even unacknowledged. Evan had learned that an important aspect of growing up is that he recognized when he had done something well.

CHAPTER XXXI
CHOOSING A MAJOR

Sleepless once again, Evan remembered that he did not experience the excitement of choosing colleges and waiting for selection letters. His father had gone to the University of Idaho-Moscow and told Evan in eighth grade that he also was going there. His father did not favor any particular major for Evan, but made it clear that he expected a bachelor's degree in the conventional four-year time span.

Since his father had taken the suspense out of college enrollment, Evan was determined to select his major carefully. He took a weekday school field trip in his junior year to the beautiful Moscow campus, an outing designed to acclimate students to the campus and its programs. While most of his fellow travelers gravitated to the student union and the field house, Evan had made two appointments with counselors in student services, concluding that if he drew one counselor who was disinterested or busy, that the second one would likely be more helpful.

"Come in, Evan, and sit down," said Mr. Browning, his first appointment, shaking Evan's hand and easing into his chair.

Immediately, the phone rang and Evan was feeling even better about having made a second appointment, but Mr. Browning, a tall, tweedy thirty-something with a well manicured goatee, disposed of the caller quickly and turned his full attention to Evan.

After relaxing Evan with small talk, he asked, "Why did you come here today?"

Evan was stunned by the directness of the question for a moment and simply stared at the counselor.

Mr. Browning continued, "You're not like other young students who come in here unprepared and distracted. You know what you want. Tell me and I'll try to help."

"I want to pick a major."

"Do you know that you will come to school here?'

"Yes."

Somewhat taken back by Evan's conviction, he hesitated for a moment and then said, "Well, let's do it."

The counselor took out a wax sheet, put it on an overhead projector, and reached for his pointer. "Let's eliminate some majors first."

Evan and Mr. Browning worked effectively together and quickly reduced the list to four: economics, English, mathematics, and pre-med.

"Any chance you'll go to law school?" asked Mr. Browning.

"A fair chance," replied Evan.

"Want to eliminate math?"

"Yes."

"Want to spend a few years in our fine science labs?"

"Not really," Evan replied.

"We are left with economics and English. Do you want to become an expert in a field in which economists become experts by the sheer force of their personality or to spend your years here in the library, reading, analyzing, and writing?"

"Looks like I'm an English major. Can I hold off choosing a minor?"

"Sure, and I would be happy to help you any time, but you are academically mature enough to go through this same process yourself in choosing a minor."

Evan agreed, shook Mr. Browning's hand gratefully, canceled his second appointment, and prowled the English department's offices and classrooms. He spent the rest of the day reading English course descriptions, sitting in the back of a big hall listening to a Chaucer lecture, and walking through the library.

Evan took some teasing on the ride home for not being seen in the student union or the domed athletic area. Increasingly, he ignored this kind of teasing because he realized that he inhabited a different dimension than most teens, but he was becoming gradually more relieved to discover that there were others in this category and that they, though few in number, tended to be responsible and fair-minded. Of continuing concern was his conclusion that those like him did not reach out to people and often recoiled during the rare instances when others reached out to them; these tendencies made developing satisfactory relationships unlikely at any age.

Accepting that a somewhat solitary existence was to be his lot in life, he went ahead with his planning for college. Using the University's course descriptions as a guide, Evan finished his last year in high school with a focus that few students possessed. By graduation, he had read many of the novels which would be assigned in his college literature classes.

CHAPTER XXXII
ENGLISH MAJOR

Evan had found a small apartment in downtown Moscow and went home most weekends. Many of the students at the University were first generation students of modest means, worked part-time jobs, and had little time for dating. Evan worked in the Instructional Technology laboratory fifteen hours per week and did not have a single date during his first two years in Moscow. Males and females alike seemed so busy that being on campus in the daytime was like being in a bustling train station with everybody running a few minutes late.

One pain-wracked night, Evan recalled that as a college student, he took the time to use reference books with graduate students that gave his term papers a depth and richness that the writing of few other undergraduate students possessed. In a Literature of the American West class, Dr. Scanlon, a mid-forties woman with leathery skin who had lived much of her life outdoors in Montana and Colorado, detained Evan after class one day, took him to her office, and said that she believed that Evan had plagiarized his term paper on railroads.

"I did not," he replied in confusion.

"Stay here for a moment," ordered Dr. Scanlon as she went next door to get her neighbor, Dr. Hughes, a male near retirement age.

The two professors sat on one side of the table and Evan on the other. Not only was it two against one, but it was two highly educated people holding all the cards against a lowly undergraduate who did not even have a pair of deuces. This inquisition symbolized all that was wrong with academia in higher education: the abuse of power versus a weak opponent without leverage.

Dr. Scanlon summarized her view and, without giving Evan a chance to respond, began shooting rapid fire questions. Evan was vague and disjointed on the first few questions, then found his rhythm and began providing background information about Western railroads, much of which neither professor was aware. The hours he had spent with Spiller and six or eight other reference sources were paying off.

Finally, Dr. Hughes asked, "Are you the undergrad who has been visiting the reference section regularly?"

"Yes. Was that wrong?" asked Evan.

"No, but is unusual. Dr. Scanlon, I believe we have a rare situation here and that this student has been outperforming your expectations."

Dr. Scanlon did not appear happy and went back to her office without saying a word. The following week Evan received his term paper through the mail with a "B" grade and no comment. Dr. Scanlon never again even looked his way, and Evan had learned the price of stepping out of bounds, even in a positive direction. If he ever had the kind of power these professors have, he promised himself, he would use it fairly.

In his junior year, Evan took a pre-teaching course which called for team planning. Evan and Ellen, an English major from Twin Falls, were team members and did some library work together. She was assertive and as attractive as she cared to be, sometimes dressing provocatively and other times like a member of a fundamentalist religious group. He impressed her with his well researched contributions and she pleased him by simply noticing him.

After a Friday afternoon planning session went into the early evening, she said to him, "Let's go get a beer."

He hesitated, so she took his arm and dragged him to the door, while asking him which bar he wanted to visit. Evan shrugged as she led him to her car and she drove him to the toughest place in town. Ellen ordered them each a beer and they sat at the end of the crowded bar. She pointed towards the women's restroom and headed there quickly.

A big drunken lumberjack came over, picked up her unoccupied chair, and turned to take it back to his table. Without thinking, Evan reached out and touched the man's arm, and the lumberjack turned and threw a big punch, which was slow enough that it gave Evan a chance to drop to the floor. The older man on the bar stool next to him never saw the punch coming and absorbed its full impact as the bar erupted. By this time, Ellen had returned and grabbed Evan roughly by the collar and dragged him out the door and to her car, just as the police were arriving. He gave her directions to his apartment.

"We've had enough excitement for tonight, but I'm going to have to keep an eye on you. Tomorrow, I'll pick you up at seven and we'll go to a movie. Pick one and if it's good, I'll buy the burgers," she said.

This did not seem to be a good time to argue, so he reached out to pat her shoulder and she turned without warning and kissed him.

"Good night, Ellen."

She just laughed and drove off aggressively, the way she did most things. They had two more dates which she planned and then disappeared from his life when the class project ended. He had no more dates before graduation.

Evan completed all his graduation requirements and for the most part enjoyed his studies, though he made a mistake by choosing teacher education rather than liberal arts. He was socially and emotionally unprepared for teaching and after staggering through his student teaching experience, never again considered teaching as a career.

CHAPTER XXXIII
GRADUATION AFTERMATH

Mr. Brinkley made arrangements for the family to attend Evan's graduation ceremony at the University; otherwise, Evan would have skipped the ritual. He did feel proud to wear his gown and to march with his fellow graduates; however, when he was handed his diploma by the Arts and Sciences Dean, it was obvious that he did not recognize Evan but seemed to know many of the other students. Evan had long since gotten used to people being oblivious to his presence, so he shrugged off this slight, without being offended.

Mr. Brinkley had arranged a lunch party without consulting Evan and invited a group of his business contacts, their wives, and their graduating children. Evan would have felt better if his father had asked him if he wanted to invite a date, a friend or faculty member, but again he was conditioned to having his wishes ignored. Evan well understood Tip O'Neil, the politician, who often said, "People like to be asked."

In his formal speech, his father introduced Evan briefly to the three dozen attendees and then proceeded to lavish praise on several of the business owners in attendance in what was clearly a business lunch rather than a graduation party. Some things were never going to change.

On the ride back, Mr. Brinkley asked, "Well, Evan, what are you going to do now?"

"I'm going to be a tech writer for Medfast. I start on Monday. I'd like to live at home until the end of the month, if that's OK."

Mr. Brinkley responded, "Sounds all right to me." In conversing with Evan, his dad rarely bothered with follow-up questions.

With no fanfare, Evan left the Brinkley house and moved into a small, partially furnished apartment in a secure, recently constructed six-apartment building near the Medfast complex. He took pride in making his first rent payment and in keeping his two rooms clean and orderly.

After he got his cell phone, Evan called his parents, gave them his address and phone number, and told them he would invite them over when "he cleaned the place up."

"No hurry," his mother responded, and both knew that the Brinkleys would not be visiting their son any time soon, if at all.

In a way he had always been on his own, because he had been irrelevant in his parent's home. He had spent his undergraduate years at Moscow in limbo, which allowed him to defer life decisions. It was now time to carve out an identity and build a life.

With his first paycheck, Evan bought a few items for the apartment, moving up a few notches from his Spartan student existence. He decided to add to his wardrobe gradually.

Evan adapted quickly to his job, since it called for him to spend hours reading and writing. He left the office politics to others and devoted his energy to polishing his job skills and learning the company.

To put muscle on his slender frame, Evan entered into a six-month contract so that he could lift weights at a nearby gym. He also liked the aerobic machines and understood the importance of the mind-body connection. When he worked out regularly, his work came easier.

He began attending a nearby Episcopal church. The minister and associates were friendly but not intrusive, respecting his private nature and believing that each member of the congregation was entitled to his/her own slant on worship. They sensed that people like Evan were easily spooked and that a casual slight for some could be traumatic for him.

During his first year at Medfast, Evan fell into a comfortable rhythm of work, exercise, and worship. With a few exceptions, people at work left him alone, realizing that he posed no threat to anyone. Though Evan had no friends or love interests, he was leading a life he understood and could manage.

CHAPTER XXXIV
GOD

Faced with an imminent exit, Evan was not the sort of person who would try to atone for a lifetime of selfishness and foolishness with a few months of spiritual devotion. On the contrary, Evan felt that many people owed him and that it was up to him to collect from a select few, one way or another. He believed it was his right to balance the scales of justice, and in that way he justified his attempts to get even with those who had treated him badly.

As a child, Evan was one of those nerdy little kids who actually paid attention in church, and because of his gullibility took much of what he heard literally. When the church building was referred to as "God's House," he wondered if God lived up in the rafters and who lived there with him. He also wanted to know if God traveled between churches like a gypsy, how He handled language barriers, and how He could be in more than one place at a time. When Evan learned the Ten Commandments, he thought it was clumsy to have God's rules separate from civil and criminal laws that man made. Evan felt it would be so much easier to know how to act if these two legal systems were folded into one. Finally, he wondered why, if people acted properly, anyone would need a lawyer.

As he grew older, he became increasingly disenchanted with churches because he observed people, including his father, using religion for their own purposes. For Evan, he saw Sunday morning as a time when townspeople congregated to sell insurance, promote a political view, or advertise a store, rather than to thank and respect a loving God. The use of God as a social tool confused the younger Evan and increasingly bothered the older Evan.

Those who twisted religion served to drive Evan further inward to find answers to spiritual questions and to construct a code of conduct.

As Evan grew older, he saw increasing numbers of people whom he did not want to resemble. Rather than trying to find God in all of those around him, Evan eliminated most people and, in the process, restricted his ability to relate to all but a small portion of the population.

As he grew into adulthood, Evan still attended church regularly but used his time there to review his week and to determine whether he had been fair and charitable to others. He was in a pew physically, but mentally, he was evaluating his behavior.

June looked upon church as an opportunity to track community news and her daughters' friends. She insisted upon being fifteen minutes early for church and standing with Evan on the right side as you entered the church vestibule, which came to be known as Brinkley's Corner. She did not miss anything that was said and churchgoers generally yielded sensitive information without a fight rather than submit to one of her cross-examinations. Most people simply came over and gave up their news before church, rather than have June track them with her inquisitive look and pressing questions. Negotiating Brinkley's Corner was regarded as simply one more obstacle to reaching your pew, such as parking your car and opening the heavy church doors.

In the vestibule, a woman once carelessly mentioned "gossip" in a loud voice and then looked June's way. June waited until after the service and cornered the unfortunate woman, lecturing her on what June maintained was an honest interest in people and proceeding to cite the numerous activities the Brinkley's had supported. She closed by asking the woman how much she had done for the church lately. The verbal assault was so effective, that the woman and her husband missed the church service on the next two Sundays.

Evan did not worry about a day of reckoning since he reasoned that he had already established his record, and that a last-minute Hail Mary was not going to change things. He had established a life pattern and if getting even with a few people at the end was going to diminish that slightly, then so be it. Nothing he had learned in the awakening he had undergone in the last months led him to conclude that he was either a bad human being or that he owed anyone anything. Since Evan was generally tougher on himself than others were, he felt he had reached a fair conclusion.

Evan did believe in a higher power but did not agree that the organized religions with which he was familiar had captured its essence. He concluded that the higher power was an uncomplicated set of desirable expectations, rather than a physical presence, and that people at life's end would be measured by their cumulative score on continuums of traits, including humility, fairness, unselfishness, and kindness.

CHAPTER XXXV
COURTSHIP

As Evan struggled through a walk one day, he pondered his pre-marriage relationship with June. Evan had heard that mothers often told their daughters to look for a husband in church. He had little idea, however, that he would appear on any woman's shopping list. Since he had not noticed any interest, he was surprised when an attractive, assertive woman named June Wilson approached him after a Sunday service and asked him if he was staying for the coffee-and-rolls breakfast the church provided. When Evan did not respond immediately, she smiled, took his arm, and steered him to the church hall. Here he was being handled again; Evan was either going to have to learn to respond more quickly or he was going to be pushed and pulled through life.

Evan was flattered to be seen with her, though, and he found that he wanted to know more about her. She was quite a package: beautiful grooming, good posture, pleasant voice, and impressive composure. June had learned a great deal in her twenty-four years.

"Would you like to join me at my place for supper?"

"Yes. Can I bring something?"

"Some wine would be nice and six o'clock would be a good time to arrive," June prompted, while giving him her address on a small sheet of paper. "A brown or green shirt would look good on you."

"OK."

He went back to his apartment and inspected his small wardrobe, finding a presentable green shirt. The wine was going to be a problem, because no liquor was sold on Sundays in this region. He only knew people in two of the other five apartments, Mrs. Shantz and the Hamiltons, and was able to borrow a bottle of vin rose from Mrs. Shantz, an elderly widow, with Evan's promise of replacing it early next week.

"I hope she's worth it," said Mrs. Shantz with a mischievous smile.

Evan blushed and did not reply as he backed out of her apartment. After a workout at the gym, he spent the rest of the day getting ready for his date. He knocked on June's door punctually at six o'clock, carrying the bottle of wine and sporting an anxious smile. She greeted him warmly, took the wine, and directed him towards a kitchen chair.

Evan poured the wine as June prepared the meal, and she put him through a comprehensive grilling which covered where he had been as a youngster, where he was now, and where he was going. In contrast to his father, she asked follow-up questions, and then followed up on those. Evan was glad when she said it was time to eat, because she had tired him and he thought he would get to rest, but her questions continued relentlessly through dinner and beyond. She wanted to know everything about his family, schooling, and plans for the future.

Finally, she reached the end of her questions and he asked, "Is it my turn now?"

"What do you want to know?"

"Why are you so interested in me?"

"Because you fit my profile."

"Profile?" questioned Evan.

"Yes. I don't like to date a man, unless there's at least a chance that we are compatible enough to marry some day."

Though somewhat afraid of the answer, he was curious enough to ask, "Do I fit?"

"You got all the way through my questions. No man has ever done that."

"Now what?" he asked.

"I'll let you know."

He did not doubt for a minute that June would let him know not just what, but where, when, and how. It was clear to him that he was about to be taken for a ride, that he was already buckled in, and that he must hang on tight. He walked to his car, knowing that someone was watching and assessing, and that it would take some time before he would be capable of sorting his jumbled thoughts.

June called two days later and said she wanted to take him to a play the following

Saturday that one of her friends had enjoyed; she insisted on purchasing the tickets herself. To prepare himself for the evening, he put on his best sports coat and slacks.

When he arrived, she sized him up and said, "Nice, but you need a better belt."

At the brief intermission, June introduced Evan to a couple she seemed to know well. "This is my friend, Evan. He works at Medfast."

So he was her friend; he could live with that. Holding his arm as she did, they appeared to be neither terribly in love nor brother and sister. Whatever her plans were, June was smart enough not to alarm or overwhelm him. She realized that Evan needed to be reeled in one small crank at a time.

Evan had discovered that June was a media consultant, occasionally appearing on daytime television shows and always having two or three projects going simultaneously. Not surprisingly, she had become a multi-tasker, who tolerated neither interruption nor dissent.

Evan did not know much about relationships but understood that they must be tested, and he wanted to test theirs. He called her and asked if she was available a week from Saturday, and June said she was, but seemed uncomfortable. He said he was planning something and wanted it to be a surprise.

"I don't like surprises," she blurted.

"You'll like this one. Wear casual clothes, tennis shoes, and a windbreaker. I'll pick you up at 11:00 AM."

"Where are we going?"

"I don't want to spoil the surprise," he cautioned her, before hanging up. He knew he was playing with fire but he had to determine where he stood in this relationship. He soon found out. She called him the next day and said that she was "unavailable" on the day of his surprise. Never again was there any talk of surprises in their relationship.

Soon after, June called him and indicated that she needed Evan to escort her to her company's dinner party on Wednesday evening. She directed Evan to go to Teddy's Tuxedo shop for measurements and gave him the time of the dinner and other details. He flinched when he saw the size of the rental bill, but he did not express his discomfort to her.

When Evan arrived at the upscale restaurant, June waved him over to their table and introduced him again as her friend. The others at their table had been drinking heavily, and because of the noise and confusion, Evan found it difficult to even listen politely, much less engage in intelligent conversation. June conducted some business, and Evan nursed a beer and sat through a round of dull speeches.

When June returned to the table, she berated Evan for looking bored and not being more engaged with their tablemates, who by this time were slurring their words and laughing foolishly.

"Don't be such a stick in the mud. Loosen up. Live a little."

She was called away on business again and he seriously considered leaving when a man at the next table dropped to the floor with a stroke. Everyone else was either drunk or oblivious, so Evan was forced to do something. He propped the man up against an overturned chair, took off the man's tie, and loosened his collar, while telling a reasonably sober woman to call 911.

A doctor with a bag materialized, patted Evan on the back, and took his place, checking vital signs and assessing his patient. Shortly after, EMS arrived and took the man away.

Before leaving, the doctor provided the restaurant necessary information and then made a point of thanking Evan by shaking his hand and pointing him out to those nearby as a "good person to have around." The incident had sobered everyone and at least two dozen company employees clapped their hands and patted Evan's back. The company president came over and shook his hand, thanking Evan profusely as June looked on in disbelief. She was not so awed, however, that she failed to hang on Evan to make sure that the president knew who her escort was. The stroke victim had transformed Evan from likely absentee to surefire hero. As the old saying goes, Evan thought, "Stuff will do for brains, if you're lucky enough."

CHAPTER XXXVI
ENGAGEMENT

Evan had often wondered why June had chosen him. On her side, June was almost certain she had found what she was looking for in a husband: good health, pliability, honesty, self control, stability, steady employment, willingness to take orders, and a college degree. Since June already had her hook in him, she needed to check one more trait before she lifted him into the boat.

June had a friend, Allison, who had given birth to an active set of twins two years ago. She asked Allison if June and Evan could visit her house and specifically the children, and they set a date. Allison greeted them warmly at the door and explained that her husband was running errands. The twins, Jimmy and Jessica, were playing in the front room with books and blocks, but stopped to inspect the visitors. Evan took a chair near the twins and spoke to each of them softly, peering directly into their big eyes. Jimmy brought one of his blocks to Evan, and Evan took it, placed it on the floor and put two blocks on top of it. Jimmy knocked the pile apart and then stacked them himself, prompting Evan to crumble the pile. So it went.

Jessica waited patiently for her turn with the visitor and brought a book to show Evan, who turned the pages and otherwise inspected the book thoroughly. He began asking her to identify objects in the book, at which time she raised her arms to sit in his lap. Evan looked questioningly at Jessica's mother, who nodded affirmatively and smiled. Jessica stayed on his lap for almost ten minutes before dropping to the floor and toddling away.

"That may have been the longest she has ever sat on anyone's lap without falling asleep," laughed Allison.

Discovering a kindred spirit in Evan, Jimmy came back and spent a few minutes on Evan's lap before starting to fall asleep.

Allison intervened and put Jimmy back on his feet, explaining, "If he sleeps now, it will be impossible to put him down for his regular nap later."

June used this moment as an opportunity to suggest that it was time for them to leave, since Evan had easily passed the test of not just tolerating, but genuinely enjoying children. It was time for June to close the deal!

June wanted Evan to be at ease when she popped the question. She knew Evan was most comfortable when they were walking, partly because he did not have to make eye contact when they were side-by-side. On a beautiful Saturday, she took him to hike with her on his favorite spot around the lake.

"We've been dating for five months, and I think it's about time to get engaged, don't you?" she said firmly, taking his hand, stopping him, and turning her to him.

"OK."

She leaned forward to be kissed, he complied, and they were engaged. She already had selected their rings and orchestrated the wedding preparations like a stage production. Again, there was nothing wrong with her decisions, other than that they were not *their* decisions. June insisted upon meeting his parents, charming his father with his favorite quality, efficiency, and his mother, with her favorite quality, lack of clutter.

June put a brief notice in the paper and mailed the announcements. When they went house hunting, they found a charming place on a cul-de-sac; though he liked the house well enough, it was obvious to him that she would accept no other. As always, it was all June, all the time!

CHAPTER XXXVII
THE WEDDING

While cleaning the kitchen one morning, Evan reflected upon his wedding day, which stood out in his mind, if only for its mediocrity. By day's end, he had come to consider himself a bit player in a forgettable production. June managed every aspect and every word of the ceremony, going so far as to give the minister a sheet of instructions. She insisted that her brother be the best man, because Evan "didn't know anyone well enough" to handle that responsibility.

They went through three rehearsals of the ceremony, though the first run-through seemed fine to all involved but June. Consequently, the ceremony itself came off as lifeless, lacking the spontaneity, imperfection, and humor which often give weddings their flavor. Increasingly, Evan had grown to envy those who shot from the hip and who did not live life according to a grand plan. Eccentrics, rebels, and creative thinkers were becoming his heroes, though he could never be like them.

The minister did a workmanlike job in conducting the ceremony. When the minister reached the "I do" portion, Evan managed a somewhat weak response and tugged anxiously at his collar. Ever the consummate performer, June more than made up for his lack of passion by gathering Evan into a spectacular Hollywood finish in the "Kiss the Bride" segment as the cameras flashed.

Her family's church was beautiful, and light streamed in through the stained glass windows to create a crystal shower. June had taped a list of occupants on each end of the well-maintained, wooden pews. There were only two pews of Brinkleys, and so June's family and friends filled up one side of the church and their overflow sat behind the outnumbered family.

Versatile to a fault, June was bride, greeter, bouncer, food and beverage manager, daughter, granddaughter, sister, parking coordinator, liaison between the families, and emcee, managing every situation without breaking a sweat or raising her voice. Because of her smothering approach and disconcerting ability to be everywhere at the same time, guests were afraid to have too much fun.

At the reception, she pulled aside one of her uncles who was mildly drunk and straightened him up quickly, though he was causing no harm. When guests laughed loudly or raised their voices, they glanced quickly over their shoulders for fear of drawing June's ire. Evan was relieved when all the guests had left the reception, and he and June went back to their home. He did not simply want solitude at the end of this day, he craved it.

On their wedding night, she informed him that they would not be having a child for one year, while they "worked out the kinks." Fully expecting her to be exhausted from managing the wedding, June surprised him by continuing relentlessly in control mode. She spent a half hour explaining how things would be done in "our" house. Though June was fair in dividing the household tasks and Evan knew that two working people had to share the workload, he would at least have liked to have been in on the discussion of why things were divided as they were. He was learning, however, that the answer to his question was simple: because June wanted them that way.

When they went to bed, Evan was tired but did not sleep well because his mind was whirling. He had not considered a military hitch as a life option, but he was now aware that that he was going to get a strong dose of military-like discipline. There was nothing he could do to change things, because with June at the helm, there was no turning aside or back.

CHAPTER XXXVIII
MARRIAGE, THE FIRST YEAR

Life around, not with June turned out to be not bad as long as you did not try to tailor it to your own tastes and needs. If you did what you were told, and made no attempt to decide, question, or alter things, life moved along rather well, but try acting as an independent adult, and life suddenly became difficult beyond description. Above all, avoid surprises, spontaneity and passion, all of which June detested, seeing them as threats to her grand scheme. She considered an invasion of her space a capital crime and built a fence around herself to warn people.

Evan lived his married life on auto-pilot, guided and controlled by June through lists, post-it notes, and short verbal commands. It was an extremely efficient arrangement but one that squeezed any fun out of their relationship. Her kisses and hugs were wonderful but only doled out after all their tasks had been completed. Lovemaking was always according to her schedule, as he discovered on the few occasions when he reached for her without being asked.

To neighbors and friends, the marriage appeared solid: a polite, well dressed working couple living in a nice house, obeying the laws, going to church, and paying their bills. They were saving money, in part, because Evan was only allowed to use their credit card for certain items and to carry no more than twenty dollars in cash. Their home was well cared for, inside and out, and they paid extra on their mortgage regularly.

They treated each other with consideration, using separate bathrooms, keeping an orderly refrigerator, handling each other's possessions respectfully, and taking phone messages carefully. Since Evan grew up in a home where laughter was rare, he hoped that marriage would bring some fun and that he could learn how to enjoy himself and perhaps even make others laugh. This was not to be. June looked at life primarily as a series of tasks to be managed in an orderly manner, not a series of relationships to be nurtured and enjoyed. She was competing with the world for mastery; so far, she was ahead on points and intended to stay that way.

When they had visitors in their home, June conducted parlor games and otherwise managed visitors and their activities. People generally had a good time in their home, partially because June selected interesting activities, but mostly because June insisted on it. Nobody could work a room like June, and she would lean on people until they were actively engaged. She had been approached by a local legislator with a keen eye for political talent, but when June discovered that she would have to pay her dues first by making telephone calls and staking yard signs, rather than being the candidate, she immediately lost interest.

June was particularly attractive, and since she was always well dressed and meticulously groomed, men noticed her. Most males, however, were smart enough to see the façade she had built around herself and recognize that a quick fling with June was not going to happen. The few who did not see the obstacle fared badly.

In their fourth month of marriage, June asked Evan to meet her downtown at a work-related, open-bar buffet supper in an insurance building. There were a number of out-of-town salesmen at this event and they had been slamming hard liquor for more than two hours before Evan arrived.

Leading this hardscrabble pack in alcohol consumption, decibels, and raw jokes was Brent, an overfed six-foot three-inch brute with a mop of curly hair, who had taken five large stickies and used one each for a letter of his first name and placed them across his purple blazer. In the noise and confusion, June was trying unsuccessfully to conduct some business with another salesman, when Brent sailed by and made the mistake of grabbing her and trying to steal a kiss. June caught him off balance and shoved him into a nearby alcove and scared him badly as she spoke firmly to him.

"My brother is a cop (of course, not true) and you've just committed sexual assault. When your case is called in criminal court, you are going to have trouble finding good legal help in this county, because my family knows everyone around here. If you aren't out that door in ten seconds, I will call my brother and have you arrested."

Though Evan had moved across the room close to June, he was thankful that he was not needed. Soundly deflated, Brent fled without looking back and June again demonstrated both her ability to handle any situation and her dislike for spontaneity, alcohol-driven or not. Evan was in strong and very safe hands, but he was being kept an eternal child.

CHAPTER XIL
FATHERHOOD

Shortly after their first anniversary, June announced it was time to build a family, and she became pregnant as if she had willed it. Continuing her power walks and excellent eating habits, June was able to continue to do most household tasks and her job during her pregnancies. Occasionally, Evan was directed to retrieve something from a top shelf or to lift a heavy object, but she was a trooper, asking for help only when clearly needed. June insisted on a woman doctor, and she drove herself regularly to see Doctor Cynthia Mapes, anticipating her questions and, for the most part, self-directing the nine months of maternity. The kind doctor could only shake her head in amazement since June was invariably right, and she let the pregnancy proceed with little coaching.

After her water broke on a warm July evening, June was still sorting wash and writing a list for Evan. She walked into the hospital, before being informed that she could go no further without sitting in a wheel chair. She pouted but complied and was pushed to the delivery room. Months ago, a test had indicated that the baby was a girl. June informed Evan that she would be called Sharon, who made her appearance within an hour after her mother reached the hospital.

Through maternity ward windows, Evan looked at his daughter in astonishment. Sharon wore a little pink hat, a night shirt, an ankle bracelet, and her mother's no-nonsense look. He was ill-prepared for how tiny her hands were and dazzled by her beauty. Standing there with another father who asked Evan which child was his, Evan pointed at Sharon. The new father next to him pointed proudly to a husky baby in a blue hat and told Evan that his son was named Matt. Evan was too overwhelmed to speak and could not take his eyes off his daughter.

June's highly efficient approach to baby management allowed Evan hours to hold his daughter and to talk with her. Sharon responded to Evan's gentleness with soft smiles and cooing, which this new father enjoyed greatly. June almost caught herself smiling a few times when she noticed how close father and daughter had become. This connection made keeping the order which she insisted upon much easier to achieve. On more than one occasion, she had to remove Sharon from Evan's arms as both slept peacefully. June was puzzled by the peace she observed in father and daughter, because she had never experienced anything like it, so she simply shook her head and went on to her next task.

Evan had similar close relationships with Mary and Cary; he was certainly closer to them than June was until they were toddlers. The girls at fifteen months or so started to gravitate towards their mother because they sensed where the strength and power was. The girls from then on went to their mother for their marching orders and to their father when they were tired or wanted a story. Evan felt privileged to play any role in their lives and was fascinated by their growth and development. June was satisfied with this arrangement, since it cemented her position as current and future family manager.

June deployed the three girls in bedrooms which she decorated and furnished. Sharon had her own bedroom and Mary and Cary shared a larger bedroom. Evan was impressed by how smoothly things went as the girls grew older; all four of them looked to June for instructions, which she always had ready.

At age eight, Mary became quite ill with a lung infection and high fever, and June insisted on taking her to the hospital for treatment. Later, when June dispatched Evan to the hospital to pick up some of Mary's clothing, Evan overheard a discussion that he was not supposed to hear.

An orderly remarked to a nurse that "if that woman (June) bosses me around one more time, I'm quitting." He went on to say that Mary got special treatment because the staff wanted her discharged ASAP because June was "getting to them all." Evidence continued to accumulate that being married to June was a decidedly mixed blessing.

As the girls reach their teen years, June cranked up her already stringent supervision a notch, seeming to anticipate problems and keeping problems small. Through a comprehensive campaign of reason and intimidation, she had managed to convince all four of them that mother definitely knew best.

Because Sharon was not easily intimidated, Sharon used reason in large doses, and she and her mother became close allies. Mary and Cary were more likely to be intimidated, so reason in their relationships was generally in short supply. They took orders and were stared down, when necessary. Mary and Cary kept their distance from their mother.

Evan's responsibilities were clearly identified. He provided transportation to schools, the library, the mall, and homes of the girls' friends. Being patient and kind, he was effective in teaching each of them to read and drive. When Sharon challenged him, he ignored her and went on teaching or stopped and waited until she settled down. Mary and Cary were less likely to challenge him but more likely to let their attention slip, prompting Evan to pause and encourage his daughters to focus. As part of Evan's teacher education training, he had tutored students with much the same result: the aggressive students challenged him and the more passive students blew him off. Some things just do not change!

He did not recall ever raising his voice to any of his daughters, and his irritation with their teen moods was mild. Evan would like to have engaged in his daughters' selection of colleges, but June had already handled that. Again, he could not fault the results. A person often is either heavily controlling or highly intelligent; June was both.

CHAPTER XL
HIS EARLY WORK YEARS

While driving, Evan frequently found himself reviewing his work years. Evan had found his writing assignments at work to be increasingly satisfying. Much of his fragile adult identity was wrapped around the brochures, reports, and plans which he prepared. His supervisor, Mr. Schaefer, rarely spoke to Evan but communicated effectively with a batch of nods, winks, and hand gestures. Holding the written work in one hand, he would nod if acceptable, and pump his fist in approval if Evan had succeeded above and beyond.

On the few occasions that Evan's work had missed expectations, Mr. Schaefer would sit at Evan's desk and circle sections that needed changes and/or point to important print references. Mr. Schaefer knew that it was important to approach workers in a unique manner; for example, he understood that Evan was easily intimidated and that the more he said to Evan, the more likely Evan would be to obsess over his supervisor's comments. Further, he noted that Evan was able to screen out diversions like attractive women, sports scores, and water cooler gossip. Mr. Schaefer felt it was his responsibility to keep Evan's life simple, so that Evan could continue to apply his superior intelligence and keen insight, without distraction.

Mr. Schaefer was responsible for preparing end-of-year evaluations for eleven employees; each employee was allotted thirty minutes for explanation and discussion. Schaefer was regarded as a stern taskmaster, and the other ten employees were on edge at this time of year; the exception was Evan, who always buried himself in his work. Prior to and during the evaluation period, these ten employees often could be found huddled in small groups and engaged in animated discussion.

When Evan did enter Mr. Schaefer's office for his evaluation at the end of the first year, his supervisor walked in front of his desk, handed Evan a copy of the evaluation, shook his hand, turned him around gently and sent him on his away. At his desk, Evan read the glowing evaluation, tucked it in his top drawer, and without a change of expression or wasted motion, resumed working.

Evan noticed when less talented employees were promoted or praised in front of others, but he understood that much of his company's success depended upon the sparkle which these employees provided and the communications network they maintained. Medical supplies were not glitzy by nature and several employees made good livings enticing people to buy Medfast's products, while Evan helped provide the print rationale for the company's supremacy and insured that the company's employees at all levels stayed on the same page. Evan did not perform on the main stage, but wrote the scripts for those who did.

Many of his co-workers envied Evan because of his discipline and independence, knowing that he had job security based upon skills, insight, and intelligence, as opposed to theirs which depended upon fragile social contacts, relations which could sour or boomerang at any time. They picked on him now and then, calling him a "strange duck," but for the most part left him alone.

Savvy workers also knew that Mr. Schaefer had Evan's back. One memorable episode found Evan being tormented by Vinny Antonelli, who challenged Evan on his way to the men's room, stepping in Evan's path no matter which way he turned. Evan finally was reduced to tears, and Vinny went back to his desk. Mr. Schaefer quickly got wind of this confrontation and took a position with his arms folded next to Vinny's desk, looking not at Vinny but straight ahead. Mr. Schaefer remained transfixed and unblinking for almost thirty minutes before returning to his office. A half hour was long enough to have Vinny sweating and twitching. After this incident, Evan's problems with others decreased markedly and with Vinny disappeared altogether. Would-be tormenters had gotten the message: leave Evan alone.

Female employees were uncomfortable with Evan because of his complete disinterest in them. They teased him occasionally but he pretended not to notice, and most women soon tired of playing this game. They also knew that Evan was capable of explaining complicated company matters, so that they could understand them. He was an easy target as someone to tease but most realized that he was more valuable as an interpreter of complex medical supply issues for them. Females and males alike were intimidated by his keen intelligence and his ability to focus.

CHAPTER XLI
HIS LATER WORK YEARS

Despite a few, short downturns during Evan's tenure, Medfast enjoyed generally good corporate health. Shortly before Evan retired, the company had 125 employees; consequently, there were always dreary mini-dramas revolving around personal problems such as gambling, divorces, and addictions. All employee problems seemingly could be traced back to one or more poor decisions, which often left Evan shaking his head as to how people could be so foolish. In fairness to his co-workers, though, Evan understood that while being married to June walled him off from personal and emotional development, it also provided insurance against poor decisions, because it left Evan with few decisions to make, risky or otherwise.

It was not discomforting for Evan that he had been with the company long enough in a non-visible capacity as to become part of Medfast's fabric, resembling institutional furniture more closely than a company spokesperson. Instead, his role gave him good cover. While many co-workers soared like eagles or crashed like falling bottles, Evan maintained a steady safe altitude with June as his pilot.

Under her direction, he had contributed regularly into a 401 (k) retirement account, which had done quite well, largely because the company matched one dollar for every two contributed by the employee. The girls each had a well-funded college account, and money was not a problem for June and Evan. Other employees tried to work a second job to supplement a life style that they could not afford; this choice often led to health problems and/or mediocre Medfast performance. Financially, Evan and June entered a comfort zone and stayed there.

With strong analytical skills and his loner work style, Evan adapted quickly to technological changes, while some co-workers tried to bluff their way through change and were quickly exposed. Since computer skills are incremental and he had worked for the company during most of its technological changes, he had become an important source of information.

The most logical move would have been to have Evan teach small classes. Mr. Davis, a human relations supervisor, after a meeting with Mr. Schaefer, offered Evan a promotion and a raise, if he would wear a part-time trainer hat.

"I tried teaching and it didn't go well," said Evan, thinking of his student teaching experience.

"We want you to share what you know with others," responded Mr. Davis. "How are we going to tap into that fine mind of yours?"

"Perhaps I could tutor one-on-one, if people are serious about learning," Evan suggested, thinking of his daughters' tutoring years.

"Thank you, Evan. You've given me an idea. Let me think about it and I'll get back to you."

So was born the Brinkley hour, an in-house Medfast term describing a visit from Evan in which he sat next to a company executive in his/her office and explained how to use the computer's potential to strengthen the company. Mr. Davis had promised that Evan would have to devote no more than one hour per appointment and have no more than one appointment per day. Further, to insure that the time was spent profitably, the executive being tutored had to send a list of questions to be covered to Evan and a copy to Mr. Davis at least twenty-four hours prior to the meeting.

The tutoring went well as the executives discovered that Evan was a great source of profitable ideas and that Evan did not care who got credit for these ideas. With copies of the preliminary questions, though, the perceptive Mr. Davis understood clearly what was happening and how Evan was helping move Medfast forward. Without a dissenting vote of the personnel committee members, Mr. Davis was able to gain approval of a nice pay raise for Evan. He called Evan into his office to give him the news.

"Evan, your tutoring is going well."

"Thank you, sir," Evan responded nervously. "I hope that..."

"No, Evan," Mr. Davis interrupted and laughed, "I'm not suggesting that we change the arrangement, but we want to give you a raise which you've obviously earned."

"Thank you, sir," Evan said flatly without changing expression or making eye contact, as he looked eagerly toward the door.

"You can go now," Mr. Davis said to a relieved Evan.

Mr. Davis looked after him as he exited and thought how unusual it was to think that this strange man was one of the company's most valuable assets. He wondered if Medfast had other employees whose contributions were yet to be discovered and he vowed to keep a sharper eye.

CHAPTER XLII
LINDY, TWILIGHT TIME

Though Lindy traveled during the week, Evan continued to see her regularly on the weekends. She would call him on Friday when she got back into town, and they let his strength dictate their activities. His pain was constant now, but it was generally dull and bearable.

If Friday was a particularly bad day for him, she would bring carry-out food to his home and they would sit and talk, until he nodded off. One wonderful Friday, he awoke to discover her sleeping but still holding him. The roles were reversed briefly, and he treasured every minute until she awakened. She kissed him gently and went home.

On Saturday, Lindy spent the day running errands and doing chores to prepare for her next week's work. He would call her late in the afternoon and if his condition warranted, they would try to catch a movie. One Saturday, Evan was feeling stronger than usual, so Lindy secured tickets to an especially good play. They held hands and lost themselves in the performance, but Evan's condition worsened and he told her at the intermission that he would have to go home. Informing her that he would take a cab home, Evan begged her to stay, but she would have none of it.

He asked her to come in the house that evening, and when seated, told her, "You don't have to do this any more. I'm a burden. This can't be any fun for you."

"If I didn't want to be with you, I would have left weeks ago," she assured him as she draped an arm around his shoulder. "I wouldn't want to be anywhere else or with anybody else."

Evan's eyes became watery as he gritted his teeth through the pain, but he still managed a smile, looking at this wonderful woman.

"This illness must exaggerate my many charms," he quipped.

On Sundays, he tried to spend the early part of the day with his daughters. They all assembled at Cary's house one Sunday, but the noise, laughter, and confusion was too much for Evan. Each Sunday thereafter, he would try to visit one family at a time. One Sunday, his illness forced him to cancel, but for the most part these visits went well.

Trying in part to make up for a lifetime of what Evan perceived as weak parenting, he encouraged the grandchildren to ask questions and make observations. Of all that was said, three questions stuck in his mind:

"Will I get sick like you before I die, grandpa?"

"Why aren't you sick on the outside, too?"

"Will we get what you have, grandpa?"

Evan would go back to his home and nap in mid-afternoon on Sundays and call Lindy when he awakened. They would eat supper at his house, watch the evening news, and then discuss her work week and his upcoming doctor's appointments. Though his energy was decreasing, he relished the routine, which validated his existence. After eight Sundays on this schedule, Evan realized that the end was near. On a Sunday evening with June, he asked her if she was going to be gone until Friday.

Looking at him closely and realizing the importance of the question, she replied, "I had planned to, but I could get back on Wednesday, if you'd like."

"If it wouldn't be too much trouble?"

"Not at all," she said. "Let me call my supervisor."

She walked into Evan's kitchen with her cell phone and made the necessary adjustments with her boss, who understood Evan's situation. She returned to Evan and gave him the OK sign with her fingers.

"Thank you. I love you in case you hadn't noticed," he said.

"I noticed, but thanks for saying so. I love you too," responded Lindy.

They looked at each other for a long time before kissing and hugging, each understanding that they may not see each other again and trying to etch an indelible picture of each other in their minds. Their love for each other was short in duration, hampered by his illness, and complicated by her travels, but true nonetheless. Each supposed that most people do not share a moment in their lives as perfect as this one.

CHAPTER XLIII
THE HOME STRETCH

After a fitful night's sleep, Evan staggered out of bed and into the kitchen early Monday morning. He called each of his daughters and asked that they keep in touch this week, because he was not feeling well. Their responses were typical: Sharon demanded more information, Mary became emotional, and Cary wanted to come over and help. By explaining that he needed to be alone today, Evan stalled all three. His breakfast toast and juice had little taste, but he knew he needed his strength, so he capped his meal with an energy drink, which he took into the back yard.

This October in the Northwest was particularly beautiful, and his trees had taken on riotous colors. He eased into a large, old swing, everybody's favorite, and pictured his family members at different ages, laughing and talking where he was presently sitting. He reflected on the early years of their marriage when it seemed as though the children would never become self-sufficient, and then the middle years of marriage when the children were on the road to self-sufficiency and seemed to mature at warp speed.

Evan did not feel that he had been cheated by life, but had come to realize that he had cheated himself. For most people, who had always been active participants in life, he assumed that being given a death sentence would be a reason to be distraught. The advantage of the forewarning he received is that it gave him a chance to say and do things that otherwise would never have been said or done. Evan had done well in balancing his scale and was pleased with his life since the cancer verdict.

Evan had a lingering regret: he had set the bar much too low. Had he asked more of the people in his life, Evan now knew he would have received more in return. In retrospect,

June could have been a world class wife, had he insisted on being a partner rather than a passenger. If he had been more forceful, he could have taught his daughters important lessons about give-and-take; Evan would thereby have added an important dimension to his daughters' lives. Had he been willing to take risks at Medfast, he could have contributed more to his company. His tutoring success proved that.

Evan had not tugged hard enough, if at all, on the ropes between himself and the people in his life. He did not understand until recently that taut interpersonal ropes were perhaps the best sign of healthy relationships. He now believed that steady give-and-take between people kept lives, communities, organizations, and even countries moving forward. When he tugged harder on his ropes recently, he and those connected to him functioned with greater purpose and achieved better results. When he pulled people towards him, communication improved, attention increased, and even humor became a possibility.

How Evan envied those who laughed, teased, and enjoyed their way through each day. He had lived his entire life without having many days where he had laughed more than twice and could not recall ever causing laughter that was not directed back at him. Evan realized now that he should have avoided blaming his parents for not giving him a sense of humor; instead, he should have made it his business to have developed one. He was slow to realize that parents do what they can, and that it is up to children to fill in the gaps.

Evan felt groggy and walked back to his back porch entrance, where he fell, passing out on the linoleum in the foyer. He slept for two hours, waking stiff and cranky. Crawling to the refrigerator, he grabbed a twelve-ounce Gatorade and chugged it without taking a breath, then ate a power bar in small chunks. Feeling somewhat better, he regained his footing but was able to move from room to room only by leaning on an object or wall.

Placing his cell phone next to him, Evan dropped into bed and slept again. Waking with a powerful thirst, he drank two glasses of water and then took a shower. Feeling better, he went to the kitchen to prepare supper, flipping on the television robotically. He wondered what he was going to watch: news shows which prepared him for the next weeks and months, when he was not going to be around; sitcoms which suggested ways to manage close relationships, though his relationships were all but completed; and cop shows and dramas which appealed to people who liked to see the bad guys caught, with the bad guys now being the least of his concerns.

Evan turned off the television and went to bed, reasoning that he would not die in bed, because sleep seemed to give him a brief burst of energy, much like an ancient battery receiving a slight charge. Waking early the next morning and turning on the radio, his pain and confusion prevented him from focusing on the words, so he switched to an easy listening music station.

His goals now were to see his daughters and to live until Wednesday evening. As Tuesday wore on, he became increasingly unsettled. In the late afternoon, he called his daughters and asked to see them one last time, requesting that all three visit at 7 PM and asking them not to bring their husbands or children.

CHAPTER XLIV
DAUGHTERS, GOOD-BYE

Evan was putting his house in order, he laughed grimly to himself, as he straightened up the kitchen and disposed of the garbage. If he played this right, he would check signals one last time and spare his daughters the unpleasantness and inconvenience of a prolonged death scene. After shaving and combing his hair, Evan drank a cola which opened his eyes and made him more alert, before arranging a blanket around him in an easy chair facing the street. Underneath the blanket, he had a hard rubber ball which he would squeeze intermittently; compressing the ball helped to mask his pain and hopefully would prevent him from frightening his daughters.

At 6:50, Sharon stepped from her car in the drive but waited outside until her sisters arrived. Unsmiling, they looked at each other and nodded without speaking, since they obviously had spoken within the past few hours.

As they approached the front door, Evan mustered the strength to call loudly, "Come in, you rascals!"

The girls laughed nervously, and the tension was broken. Evan could not have been prouder; he had made adults laugh once again, and better yet, his daughters were enjoying his little joke. As they settled in their chairs and inspected their father, who was sitting up straight, he looked back at them, wearing a smile of contentment that they had seldom seen.

Evan proceeded to review the various details of his looming death and its aftermath in a businesslike manner. All four understood that if they managed his death effectively, Evan's grandchildren would view death as a natural end to a life cycle. Conversely, if the adults became hysterical or anxious, they might convey the notion that death is something to be feared.

"OK, we have a handle on the details. What questions do you have?"

"Surely we can do something, Dad," insisted Sharon.

"What would that be?" Evan asked.

"We could get everybody together," suggested Mary.

"To watch me die?" laughed Evan.

"Isn't there something the doctors can do?" asked Cary.

"They've offered me pain medication, but the cancer is too powerful. The best thing you can do for me is to go home and hug everybody. Right now, I'm getting sleepy," he said as he gave the ball a hard squeeze. "I'll last at least another week," he lied.

The girls would not leave without promising him to be awake for a nurse visit at 2 PM tomorrow. He stiffly walked to the door and held out his arms for a group hug, something he had never done before. Evan was just not a huggy guy, and his daughters hesitated briefly before all three went to him and hugged away. The considerable pain and discomfort he was experiencing were easily outweighed by this wonderful expression of their love for him. He must count for something, he concluded.

He looked fondly at his daughters as they walked to their cars, thinking it ironic that it took a terrible disease to bring them so delightfully close to him. He stumbled back to his chair and fell asleep, appreciating the view and wincing from the pain. Waking later, he crawled back to bed after drinking a bottle of Gatorade.

Wednesday was a struggle from the moment Evan opened his eyes. His balance and vision had been compromised, and the dull pain was punctuated by knife-like jolts. He was determined not to be home for the nurse's 2 PM visit. Bolstered by an energy drink, Evan prepared to take a short drive. His vision had improved and Evan drove slowly and safely to the base of a mountain.

CHAPTER XLV
MOUNTAIN TOP

Evan drove slowly up a winding gravel road to the mountain top and parked off-road in a cluster of bushes. Though hallucinating and fatigued, he did not want to die on his front seat. Gathering himself, he sat up straight and looked inward for strength during his last few hours. Evan placed a letter, which he had composed days ago, on the dash board. It read:

"My daughters, sons-in-law, grandchildren, and Lindy- If love for a person is a mixture of respect, concern, awe, and gratitude, be assured that I love you all. I envy each of you because of the confidence and joy with which you lead your lives. I am proud of the identities you have forged for yourselves and the high regard in which others hold you. Though you all share some qualities with me, each of you, in my view, is more complete, interesting, and vital than I.

To my daughters, I have found your ability to thrive astonishing, since you did it without inspiration from a strong father. I admire the manner in which you treat one another. Your ability to focus upon goals and to persist is commendable. I am glad that you have shown that you love me but do not need me; fortunately, we all understand the difference.

To my sons-in-law, I am pleased that you married into our family, that you act responsibly, and that you are kind to my grandchildren. The bond which we share, a love for my daughters, is complex and powerful. Though you have intimidated me, each in your own way, I have tried to make you welcome. Please do not let up for any reason. You are doing fine!

To my grandchildren, I regret my inability to show you how much I care for you. You are fascinating creatures, much more interesting than any book or movie. Do not think that I missed your growing and changing, but I just did not make a fuss about it. Maybe after I pass, I will still be able to follow your progress. I certainly hope so. Continue to assert yourselves so that you let others know what you stand for and why. Refuse to inherit my chief regret: that people did not know or care who I am.

To Lindy, I will be eternally grateful for your kindness, patience, and love. You have drawn forth a dimension, a power in me, which I did not know I possessed. You have provided a sense of fulfillment, which would otherwise not have been possible. Everyone loves you, in large part, because you are so comfortable with yourself. How fortunate I was to have found and loved you, however briefly. Consider our relationship as a mere chapter and go on to meet someone who deserves you.

Thanks to all of you for sharing life with me! Do not interpret my suicide as a reflection upon any of you. I do not want to bother with hospitals and tubes, because I'd much rather die outdoors. It's simply time for me to go!"

Evan struggled slowly up the mountain trail, while staring unblinkingly at the sun. He rationed his scant lingering energy to reach a lengthy, recessed ledge facing the setting sun.

Pausing briefly to admire a curious snowshoe rabbit in his path, he smiled broadly, causing the rabbit to approach him and scratch one of Evan's boots. The rabbit retreated a short distance and then turned to take another look, seeming to understand that Evan was in distress. As the floppy creature hopped around a bend in the trail, Evan slumped clumsily onto the ledge and checked his watch.

There was one hour remaining before sunset, when he planned to topple from the ledge to the boulders far below. As he shifted to make himself comfortable, Evan sipped from a flask of brandy, which he had stored in his coat pocket. He had never felt so relaxed. Though very alone, he was at peace and ready to die.

Concurrently, Evan's GPS had led Lindy and his daughters to the bush-encircled car. Lindy furtively gathered the suicide note and put it in her pocket. Guessing its contents, she vowed never to show it to anyone.

Using hand gestures, the foursome fanned out and quickly spotted Evan. They approached the ledge and stopped, looking at one another inquiringly. Each sister nodded at Lindy, who smiled and assumed a sitting position close to Evan. By looking over her shoulder and gesturing, she invited his daughters to sit close by.

"You didn't really think that we were going to let you die by yourself, did you?" Lindy asked Evan.

"I hate to be a bother," replied Evan in a raspy voice.

"Sarah and Rachel said 'good-by,' dad. They seemed more proud than sad," Sharon reported.

"Ned simply wanted to know where you were going," Mary added. "We'll answer his question tonight."

"Monte said that he would request a minute of silence on his show for you, dad. I'm not sure he can be quiet that long," Cary laughed, and the others joined in.

The five of them then sat motionless for twenty minutes; time seemed to stand still, as though in respect for the dying man. The sun was dropping rapidly and providing a surreal, half-light. Despite his pain and fatigue, Evan turned to each and smiled weakly, thinking how lucky he was to die in a place where he wanted to be, surrounded by people he loved. He need not tumble down a cold hard mountain for his exit, but could relax in the warmth and love provided by four fine people.

Evan had made great strides in balancing the scales during the last few months and had come close enough to erase many misgivings, fears which had festered within him most of his life. He had lived long enough to feel a lifetime of regrets melting away. By redefining himself, moreover, Evan had enabled others to understand his values and intentions, a meager legacy perhaps, but better than the void of a few short months ago.

"There's hope for me yet," he laughed to himself without bitterness.

Lindy nestled him in her arms carefully. Evan used the last of his energy to hug Lindy and direct his gaze proudly over her shoulder at his sobbing daughters. He then inhaled deeply and turned his head, dying as he had lived most of his life, quietly and gently, but alone no more.